101

ROMANTIC GETAWAYS

101
ROMANTIC GETAWAYS

Bounty Books

Publisher: Polly Manguel
Project Editor: Emma Hill
Designer: Ron Callow/Design 23
Picture Researcher: Emma O'Neill
Production Manager: Neil Randles

First published in Great Britain in 2010 by Bounty Books,
a division of Octopus Publishing Group Limited
Endeavour House, 189 Shaftesbury Avenue, London, WC2H 8JY
www.octopusbooks.co.uk
Reprinted 2011
An Hachette UK Company
www.hachette.co.uk

Text previously appeared in:
501 *Must-Visit Destinations*
501 *Must-Visit Cities*
501 *Must-Visit Natural Wonders*
501 *Must-Visit Islands*

A CIP catalogue record is available from the British Library

ISBN: 978-0-753719-36-7

Printed and bound in China

Please note:

We now know that political situations arise very quickly and a city or country that
was quite safe a short time ago can suddenly become a 'no-go' area. Please
check with the relevant authorities before booking tickets and travelling if you
think there could be a problem.

The seasons given in this book relate to the relevant hemisphere. Be sure to
check that you visit at the correct time.

Contents

Introduction

We all need a little romance in our lives, but in today's busy world, time at work usually takes precedence over time off. Mobile phones and computers ensure that we can always be reached, and this makes our precious spare time more important than ever. Relationships need nurturing, and a romantic getaway is one of the best ways to re-affirm the bond between yourself and your lover.

One of several dictionary definitions of romance is 'a mysterious, exciting, sentimental or nostalgic quality, especially one associated with a place', and all of us have happy memories attached to different parts of the world. It might be the place where we first met our partner, where a proposal of marriage was made or accepted, where we went on honeymoon, or simply where we once spent a romantic weekend away.

People's ideas of a romantic getaway are as diverse as people themselves, ranging from a long weekend at a chic boutique hotel in a historic city like Paris or Venice, or spending a week staying in a beautifully appointed houseboat on Lake Dal in India, camping by a lake in the Queen Charlotte Islands or relaxing beside the ocean on the island of Bali. This book is a guide to some of the wonderful places in the world that you and your lover

can enjoy together.

Whether you decide to travel to an exciting destination that is completely new to you both, or possibly to introduce your loved one to somewhere that is special to you, you'll be creating a shared romantic memory for the future, whilst exploring new places, enjoying new experiences and discovering more about one another.

Imagine the pleasure of finding yourself in the walled city of Taroudant in Morocco, with its glorious backdrop of the snow-capped Atlas Mountains, or listening to Fado singers in a little bar in Lisbon. You could explore 'Old Charleston' with its fabulous colonial architecture, or marvel at hundreds of historic temples in Kyoto. Perhaps you just feel like a quick weekend away in Scotland, eating oysters at Loch Fyne and enjoying the magnificent scenery.

If time is of the essence, there are many lovely places you can visit just for a couple of days, but this book also features exotic, far-flung destinations where you could easily spend a few weeks or more. Within a few hours you could be beachcombing in the Maldives, snorkelling in the Philippines, wandering around the bustling Christmas Fair in Prague, drinking mulled wine to help ward off the cold or maybe standing hand in hand somewhere in Iceland, gazing awe-struck at the Aurora Borealis...What are you waiting for?

7

ROMANTIC GETAWAYS IN
EUROPE

Stockholm

Located on the east coast of Sweden at the mouth of Lake Mälaren, Stockholm is widely renowned for its natural beauty. The city is built on a group of fourteen islands in the Stockholm Archipelago, making a wonderful location for this, Sweden's capital city.

The Swedish statesman Birger Jarl erected a fortress on the small island of Gamla Stan in 1252 to help defend the narrow passage of water leading from the Baltic to Lake Mälaren. It is said that he chose the spot by pushing a log into the water to see where the currents would take it ashore, showing him the best

POPULATION:
818,000 (2009)
WHEN TO GO:
May to October
DON'T MISS:
Kungliga Slottet – the Royal Palace of Stockholm and the king's official residence.
Gamla Stan – the old town; an area of medieval alleyways and cobbled streets dating back to the 13th century.
Stadshuset – the red-bricked City Hall which dominates Kungsholmen.
Vasamuseet – this maritime museum displays the only fully intact 17th century ship ever salvaged.
YOU SHOULD KNOW:
In winter there are only six hours of daylight per day.

location for a harbour for returning ships. The city's name derives from this spot: log (stock) and islet (holm). The settlement that grew up around the fortress eventually became the Stockholm of today. By the middle of the fifteenth century it became the capital of the Scandinavian kingdom, which then encompassed modern-day Sweden, Norway, Denmark, Finland, Iceland and Greenland. The first independent King of Sweden, Gustav Vasa, was crowned in 1523 so Stockholm became home to the royal family as it still is today.

Stockholm's old town is on the island of Gamla Stan and still retains its medieval street plan, with

The skyline of Stockholm at dusk

Stortorget Square

buildings in almost every western European style. The city is fresh and colourful as most houses are still painted in their original colours: seventeenth-century buildings are red, eighteenth-century buildings are yellow, more recent buildings are off-white or grey.

Stockholm boasts several royal palaces which are interesting to explore. The largest is the Baroque Drottningholm, originally built in the late sixteenth century. The palace is still the private residency of the Swedish royal family, but it is also a popular tourist attraction with wonderful gardens. There are over 70 museums in the city. The National Museet has a wide range of fine art, with 16,000 paintings (some by Rembrandt) and 30,000 other works. The Modern Museet features more contemporary works, including those by Picasso and Dalí. The Nordiska Museet is an ethnographical museum dedicated to the culture of Sweden, while Vasamuseet has the famous reconstruction of an ancient ship.

LEFT: A couple wander through the streets of Stockholm.

*Twilight in the
Lofoten Islands*

Lofoten Islands

West of mainland Norway, the Lofoten Islands lie more
than 67° north of the equator, within the Arctic Circle.
Despite this, they have a relatively mild climate
because of the warm waters of the Gulf Stream.

There are five main islands – Austvågøy, Gimsøya,
Vestvågøy, Flakstadøya and Moskenesøya – and three
smaller ones – Vaerøy, Røst and the tiny islet of
Vedøy. They are mountainous, with wooded hillsides
and are fringed with pretty bays and beautiful white,
sandy beaches.

The islands are surrounded by rich waters that
support vast colonies of breeding seabirds, including
puffins, kittiwakes, razorbills, red-necked phalaropes

and Arctic terns, as well as white-tailed sea eagles. Rare birds like capercaillie and black grouse can sometimes be spotted. In summer, sperm whales can be found offshore, while orca follow the herring to this area in early autumn. Seals and otters can also be seen and there are moose on Austvågøy.

One of the biggest deepwater coral reefs, the 40-km (25-mi) long Røst Reef is just west of Austvågøy and off the coast of Moskenesøya lies the vast whirlpool, the Maelstrom.

The spectacular ruggedness of these islands makes them popular with climbers and hikers, and the beautiful coastline is a favourite destination for cyclists. In midsummer, this beautiful area becomes even more magical, as for more than seven weeks, the sun remains above the horizon.

WHAT IS IT?
A northerly archipelago of surprising beauty.
HOW TO GET THERE:
By ferry or air from Bodø, ferry from Narvik or by road via Narvik.
WHEN TO GO:
Late May to early July for the midnight sun; the best weather is from April to September.
NEAREST TOWN:
Narvik 140 km (90 mi)
DON'T MISS:
The midnight sun
YOU SHOULD KNOW:
The sun does not rise for weeks in midwinter.

The Midnight Sun

WHAT IS IT?
A period of time when the sun never sets.

HOW TO GET THERE:
To reach Utjoki, Finland's most northerly town, fly to Ivalo and then travel by road on the E75.

WHEN TO GO:
16 May to 27 July at Utjoki

NEAREST TOWN:
Utjoki is 165 km (102 mi) north of Ivalo on the E75.

DON'T MISS:
Look out for special summer concerts held outdoors at night.

There can be fewer more romantically appealing destinations than the 'land of the midnight sun'. But where exactly is this sunshine state? Paradoxically, it is to be found in the chilly polar regions. It's a phenomenon that occurs both north of the Arctic Circle and south of the Antarctic Circle. But as there are no permanent settlements south of the Antarctic Circle, most midnight sun seekers head north.

For six months of the year the earth's north pole is tilted towards the sun. Close to the summer solstice – 21 June – this inclination is at its maximum, and the sun shines directly on the North Pole and down to a latitude of 66°34' – the Arctic Circle. If you travel north of this line at this time, you will see the sun dip towards the horizon, but not slip below it.

More than a quarter of Finland lies above the Arctic Circle, making it a perfect place to experience this magical phenomenon. In fact, at Finland's northernmost town, Utjoki, the sun does not set for a period of 73 days during summer.

Many visitors can find it difficult to sleep when the natural pattern of day and night is so disturbed. But the locals seem to revel in the experience, and an almost festive spirit breaks out throughout Finland.

This reaches a climax with the midsummer celebrations. Everywhere is decorated with birch branches and flowers and midsummer bonfires – called *kokko* – are lit. It's a time of great celebration.

When you have had enough of partying, a walk beside a beautiful lake at midnight, among the soft shadows cast by a low and luminous sun will provide an experience never to be forgotten.

YOU SHOULD KNOW:
Refraction of sunlight makes it possible to experience the midnight sun up to 80 km (50 mi) south of the Arctic Circle for a few days each year.
Mosquitoes are a nuisance during the summer in northern Finland.

The midnight sun over Lake Inari

The Aurora Borealis

The aurora borealis is Nature's very own lightshow, a shimmering stream of coloured light that suffuses the night sky. Visually stunning, part of an aurora's beauty lies in its ephemeral nature. You can never be sure when you will see one and you can never be sure what kind of display you will witness. Sometimes an aurora can be a disappointingly monochrome, diaphanous cloud. At others a pulsating psychedelic curtain of colours.

This remarkably sci-fi phenomenon has an equally remarkable sci-fi explanation. It occurs when electrically charged particles, travelling at speeds of up to 1,200 km (750 mi) per second on the solar wind, are captured by the earth's magnetic field. As these particles are drawn down towards the poles they hit the ionosphere and

The Aurora Borealis over Lake Thorisvatn

collide with the gases in the atmosphere. These collisions produce photons – light particles that glow red, green, blue and violet. The result is a shimmering sky show known as the aurora australis in the southern hemisphere and the aurora borealis, or northern lights, in the north.

Auroras appear over the poles in what are described as auroral ovals. These ovals dip further south when the solar winds are stronger, but most auroras are seen at latitudes higher than 65°N – which includes all of Iceland.

Viewing is best on crisp clear evenings in winter, away from the glare of city lights, when the nights are long and dark. Although visually spectacular, the light of an aurora is dimmer than starlight – so if you cannot see any stars you are unlikely to see the northern lights.

WHAT IS IT?
An electric display of atmospheric fireworks.
HOW TO GET THERE:
To see the aurora borealis in Iceland you must fly to Reykjavic.
WHEN TO GO:
The best months are October to March, late autumn being the best time of all.
NEAREST TOWN:
Get as far away from town and its light pollution as possible.
DON'T MISS:
Haukadalur Valley, 193 km (120 mi) north of Reykjavic, the home of the Great Geysir.
YOU SHOULD KNOW:
Aurora 'forecasts' can be found on the internet, search for 'spaceweather'. For much of the summer the Icelandic sky never really gets dark enough to see the aurora.

Copenhagen

Wonderful, wonderful . . . Thanks to the Danny Kaye
song, you know the rest. Copenhagen is a city that
should be visited at least once in a lifetime, because
the Danish capital has special charm. Denmark has

the world's oldest monarchy, and the royal family lives
in the middle of the city at the Amalienborg Palace.
Don't be surprised to see Queen Margrethe out and
about, as the royals are famously egalitarian.

A sense of history is everywhere as you stroll
through cobbled squares and narrow streets lined
with old buildings, before finding the vast City Hall

*Copenhagen's picturesque
waterside bars and
restaurants*

Square, bounded on one side by the renowned Tivoli Gardens with Strøget (the straight), Europe's longest pedestrian shopping street, on the other. The square was constructed around 1900 in romantic style and

POPULATION:
521,000 (2009)
WHEN TO GO:
Explore Copenhagen in summer, when the weather is pleasant and evenings are light and long.
DON'T MISS:
The spectacular Øresund Bridge, which opened in 2000 and connects Copenhagen to Malmø in Sweden.
Gefion Fountain, Copenhagen's largest monument showing the goddess Gefion ploughing with four oxen, which has become a wishing well.
The Church of our Saviour in Christian's Harbour, with an extraordinary golden staircase winding up the outside of the spire.
Rosenborg Castle, in the centre of Copenhagen, a grand summerhouse containing the Danish royal collections, including the crown jewels.
Free entertainment in the late afternoon and evening, when a variety of street performers come out to play on the Strøget.
YOU SHOULD KNOW:
Quite a few of Denmark's 40 cricket clubs are in Copenhagen.

The elaborate hotel and restaurant Nimb

revamped when Copenhagen was Cultural Capital of
Europe in 1996. Walk down the broad Strøget and
find Gammel Square, with an exquisite bronze
fountain erected in 1608, then take a break at an

open-air café in Gråbrødre Square in the heart of this trendy shopping area.

There are excellent green parks in Copenhagen, and the Tivoli pleasure gardens offer all sorts of entertaining experiences (especially for those who like roller coasters). You must not miss the Little Mermaid, sculpted by Edward Eriksen in 1913, and doomed to sit on her rock in Copenhagen harbour for 300 years before entering the human world (just a couple of centuries to wait, then). She isn't lonely, though, with a million visitors a year.

The New Harbour (Nyhavn, built in the 17th century) is a picturesque waterside area, with mouth-watering restaurants and lively bars. Danish fairy-tale author Hans Christian Andersen lived here for some years. It serves as a starting point for water tours that give a wonderfully different view of this special city.

A sentry guards the Royal Palace.

Salzburg

Salzburg, with its world-famous baroque architecture, has one of the best-preserved city centres in the German-speaking world, and was listed as a UNESCO World Heritage Site in 1997. It is the fourth largest city in Austria, set between the Salzach River and the Mönchsberg in a wonderful mountainous area at the northern boundary of the Alps. The mountains to the south of the city make a fine contrast to the rolling plains to the north. The closest alpine peak – the Untersbergat at 1,972 m (6,470 ft) – is only a few kilometres from the city centre and makes a fine backdrop to the beautiful architecture.

Salzburg started out as a Roman town; the first Christian kingdom was established here by St Rupert in the late seventh century. During the following centuries, the Archbishops of Salzburg became more and more powerful and were given the title of Prince of the Holy Roman Empire. The 17th-century baroque cathedral, the Salzburger Dom, is one of several wonderful churches in the city. Dedicated to Saint Rupert of Salzburg, this is where Mozart was baptized.

Mozart was born in Salzburg, a fact which is impossible to miss when visiting. The city was not generous towards him during his lifetime but it does its level best to make the most of him now. Everywhere you go his music is being played, and there are two Mozart museums and even chocolate balls called Mozart Kugeln.

The Hohensalzburg Fortress was built for the prince-archbishops. It sits sedately on Festungberg Hill and is one of the largest medieval castles in Europe. It is fascinating to see the lavish lifestyle that was led here, but perhaps even better to see the truly astonishing views from the fortress over

POPULATION:
150,000 (2007)
WHEN TO GO:
May to June, or September to October
DON'T MISS:
The Mozart museums. Views from the Hohensalzburg Fortress. The Residenz - this Baroque palace is one of the most important historic buildings of Salzburg. The current building dates back to around 1600 when Prince Archbishop Wolf Dietrich von Raitenau made major changes to the original Residenz buildings.
Schloss Hellbrunn - an early Baroque castle built in the early 17th century. The castle is also famous for its watergames held in the grounds in the summer months. These games were conceived by Markus Sittikus as a series of practical jokes to be performed on guests!
A horse-drawn carriage ride around the city.
YOU SHOULD KNOW:
Salzburg is the birthplace of Mozart.

NEXT: The Hohensalzburg Fortress dominates the skyline as it protects the town.

25

A lovely wrought iron shop sign on Getreidegasse

the Alps and the city. On the other side of the river, the Schloss Mirabell was built in 1606 by Prince-Archbishop Wolf Dietrich for his mistress. It is surrounded by lovely formal gardens. The marble hall is covered with Baroque reliefs and lit by magnificent chandeliers.

Vienna

No Grand Tour of Europe is complete without seeing Austria's capital, where people still dance the night away to the haunting strains of Strauss waltzes. This fine city sits astride the 'Blue Danube' and in 2001 the old city centre became a UNESCO World Heritage Site, reflecting its historical importance.

Sacher Torte in Sacher Café

POPULATION:
1,680,000 (2009)

WHEN TO GO:
Vienna is a year-round destination but some attractions (like the Spanish Riding School and Vienna Boys' Choir) take a summer break.

DON'T MISS:
The Hofberg, an old treasury that holds the imperial jewels of the Hapsbury dynasty.

Hundertwasser House, an amazing modern apartment building with a grass roof and trees growing out of the windows.

The museum quarter in magnificent converted imperial stables, with a number of different museums including the Museum of Modern Art.

The Art Nouveau Anchor Clock, forming a bridge between two buildings in Hoher Markt, Vienna's oldest square.

Rococo Belvedere Palaces in their park setting, with collections of Austrian paintings and a stunning alpine garden (best in spring).

A panoramic view from the top of the soaring 352-m (1,155-ft) high Danube Tower with its revolving café-restaurant.

YOU SHOULD KNOW:
Sigmund Freud discovered what makes us tick in Vienna.

Vienna was at the heart of the medieval Holy Roman Empire, and later the mighty Hapsburg Austro-Hungarian Empire. Reminders of the city's illustrious past are everywhere – from the Imperial Palace itself to the Hapsburg burial vault and palaces of Belvedere and Schönbrunn, the latter home to Europe's oldest zoo. Indeed, Vienna has many famous sights, including the Spanish Riding School, St Stephen's Cathedral and the Ring Boulevard with its imposing public buildings. Then, of course, there's the Prater pleasure garden, boasting more than 250 attractions dominated by the giant ferris wheel that featured in the iconic Orson Welles film *The Third Man.*

With many parks and open spaces, Vienna is one of the 'greenest' cities in Europe. It is also renowned for

culture, with splendid theatres, an opera house, museums and a musical tradition that goes far beyond those stirring Strauss Viennese waltzes, with Beethoven and Mozart amongst illustrious former resident composers. Adolf Hitler also lived here, from 1907 to 1913, trying and failing to enter the Academy of Fine Arts. But he's no more than an unhappy memory, and today's visitors can not only sample the city's traditional and modern architecture and many cultural opportunities, but also enjoy the fine food, vibrant café society and nightlife for which the city is justly famous.

To enjoy Vienna at its most laid back, a visit to Danube Island is a must, with its countless bars, restaurants, night clubs, sports opportunities and lovely sandy beach.

Feeding birds in front of Schloss Schonbrunn.

31

Switzerland's high alpine meadows

The high meadows of the Alps remain some of the most unspoiled landscapes in Europe. They are internationally important for the unique groups of plants they contain. Among the best areas are the Parc Naziunal Svizzer – Switzerland's only national park – near Engadin in the east, around Wengen in the Bernese Oberland and in the area around the Matterhorn in the south. Under feet of snow during winter, it is amazing that any delicate plants survive here, but in early summer, watered by the melting snow, a riot of flowers appears: blue and yellow gentians, lady's slipper orchids, the rare edelweiss and bellflowers carpet the dry meadows for a brief period. Up here, no fertilizers are used and these tiny plants grow as they have for thousands of years. Even higher up, wet

Fog rises from the valley beneath an alpine meadow between Grimmels and Il Fuorn in Switzerland's only national park.

meadows, small lakes with ice-cold water and bogs are fed by water from the melting glaciers. One of the most famous tarns – lakes that form in the base of glacial cirques – is the Schwarzsee below the Matterhorn.

The scenery in these areas is, of course, spectacular, as they are dominated by the mountains above with views over the forests and valleys below.

Wildlife that may be spotted within or from these meadows and the high slopes above includes marmots, chamois, wild goats, ibex and elk. In the national park, golden eagle and reintroduced Egyptian vulture may be seen. The flower-meadows attract a wonderful array of butterflies. Up around the moraines of glaciers, a variety of rare birds such as alpine accentors, alpine choughs, and snow finches, ring ouzels and water pipits may be seen.

WHAT IS IT?
A unique landscape, filled with flowers and wildlife.
HOW TO GET THERE:
By hiking in the areas below the glaciers.
WHEN TO GO:
Early summer

POPULATION:
117,000 (2006)
WHEN TO GO:
May to October
DON'T MISS:
A canal trip.
The Groeninge Museum houses a wide range of Renaissance and Baroque masters, masterpieces of Flemish Expressionism and many items from the city's collection of modern art.
The Memling Museum formerly the Sint-Jans Hospitaal (Hospital of St. John), where the earliest wards date from the 13th century. Nowadays visitors come to see typical medieval hospital buildings filled with furniture and other objects that illustrate their history, as well as the magnificent collection of paintings by the German-born artist Hans Memling.
The Church of Our Lady; a beautiful medieval building with a brick spire of 122m (400 ft).
The Beguinage (the Market Place).
YOU SHOULD KNOW:
Chocolate, lace and beer are specialities of the city.

Bruges

Bruges, the capital city of the West Flanders area of Flemish-speaking Belgium, is one of the most beautiful and best-preserved medieval cities in Europe. Its historic centre has been designated a UNESCO World Heritage Site. Known as Brugge by the locals, the city is criss-crossed by canals edged with cobbled streets and pretty gabled houses.

During the eleventh century, wool became an important industry in Bruges, and there were strong trade links with England and Scotland's wool-producing districts. English tradesmen introduced Norman grain and Gascon wines to the city. By the late thirteenth century Bruges was the main link to Mediterranean trade. This opened not only the trade in spices from the Levant, but introduced commercial and financial techniques to Bruges which resulted in a

The reason why Bruges is known as the 'Venice of the North' can be seen here.

35

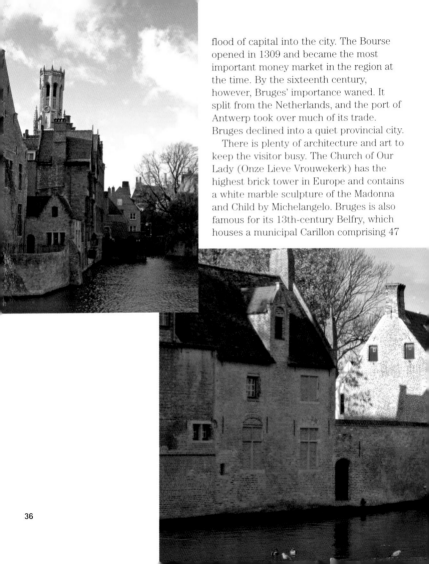

flood of capital into the city. The Bourse opened in 1309 and became the most important money market in the region at the time. By the sixteenth century, however, Bruges' importance waned. It split from the Netherlands, and the port of Antwerp took over much of its trade. Bruges declined into a quiet provincial city.

There is plenty of architecture and art to keep the visitor busy. The Church of Our Lady (Onze Lieve Vrouwekerk) has the highest brick tower in Europe and contains a white marble sculpture of the Madonna and Child by Michelangelo. Bruges is also famous for its 13th-century Belfry, which houses a municipal Carillon comprising 47 bells. The city still employs a full-time bell ringer who gives recitals. The Basilica of the Holy Blood (Heilig Bloed Basiliek) is another of the city's famous churches; it contains a phial said to contain the blood of Christ. The Groeninge Museum displays Flemish and Belgian paintings spanning six centuries, including works by Hans Memling and Jan Van Eyck, who lived and worked here. Don't forget to enjoy the open spaces of this beautiful city. Take a boat trip on the canals or just sit in a café and sip one of the 350 or more beers for which Belgium is famous. *Moules frites* and chocolate are Belgian specialities well worth indulging in.

The architectural styles of Bruges, though buildings alongside canals, can be diverse. From medieval houses to beautiful churches, from modern dwellings to a grand Italian style that shows off the wealth of the original owners (above).

Ghent

POPULATION:
233,000 (2006)
WHEN TO GO:
The unique medieval
atmosphere of Ghent is best
appreciated in warm
summer sunlight.
DON'T MISS:
The stunning Ghent
Altarpiece in St Bavo
Cathedral entitled *The
Adoration of the Mystic
Lamb,* largely attributed to
Jan van Eyck.
Picturebook Gravensteen
Castle, the 'castle of the
counts' rebuilt in
1180, with its collection of
torture instruments.
The spectacular Ghent
flower show – but plan
ahead, because it only
happens every five years.
The ancient city roofscape
seen from the top of the
90-m (295-ft)
belfry tower.
The 10-day Ghent Festival,
at the end of July, for free
music, parties, fireworks,
street theatre and markets.
YOU SHOULD KNOW:
Ghent bakers sell a bun
called a *mastle,* said to
immunize against rabies.

Try not to wear out the camera in Ghent, where lovers of romantic architecture tend to get over-excited. St Armand founded abbeys here in the 7th century but this settlement, at the confluence of the Scheldt and Lys rivers, was pillaged by Vikings in the 9th century. It recovered to become, until the 13th century, a major European city second only to Paris.

This is one of several splendid medieval towns in

Belgium that have survived the ravages of time and war – the very best of them say proud locals, with good reason . . . Ghent has more listed structures than the rest of Belgium put together. It is impossible to remain unmoved by so many seriously beautiful old buildings, lanes, cobbled streets and beautiful waterways, all providing a showcase of medieval wealth and success based on wool imported from England. The run of guild houses known as the Graslei along the old waterfront is ultra-scenic. There are

Guild houses line the waterfront in Ghent.

many churches, with St Jacob's and St Nicholas' being particularly noteworthy. Three *béguinages* (which housed orders of nuns), together with the belfry and adjacent cloth hall, are UNESCO World Heritage Sites. The trio of ancient towers that dominate the city's skyline belong to St Bavo Cathedral, St Nicholas and the belfry. A view that should not be missed is that from the Grasburg Bridge by night, looking towards the floodlit St Michael's Church.

There are fine restaurants, interesting shops and pavement cafés aplenty, but Ghent is really about culture. In addition to picturesque buildings, it has excellent museums and lively annual festivals, though a reminder of the city's commercial past and continuing present is provided by a large port to the north of the city, with access to the sea via the River Scheldt.

A view of the medieval heart of the city over the Lys River from St Michielsbrug with the 12th-century castle, Gravensteen, in the background.

Carcassonne

This is a tale of two cities in the Languedoc – Carcassonne (the walled city on a rocky outcrop) and . . . Carcassonne (the modern city). Actually,

Carcassonne at night

41

POPULATION:
48,000 (2008)

WHEN TO GO:
July, for the Cité Festival, with performances held in the extraordinary open-air theatre in the old city.

DON'T MISS:
Jacobins' Gate – built on the site of one of the lower town's four 13th-century gates in 1779.

The Memorial House, an ancient merchant establishment where poet Joë Bousquet lived – he was wounded and paralysed in 1918, and his house is now a museum and cultural centre.

St Vincent's Church, begun in the 13th century – a fine example of 'Languedoc Gothic' architecture with a rich interior.

The harbour area on the Canal du Midi – the original canal ran just outside the town, but was brought into Carcassonne between 1787 and 1810.

The André Chénier Garden, created in the 1820s around a memorial to executed King Louis XVI following the restoration of the French monarchy.

St Michael's Cathedral, begun in the 13th century, updated in the 17th century, restored in the 19th century – and still impressive.

YOU SHOULD KNOW:
St Gimer's Church is one of only three ever built by architect Viollet-le-Duc, who restored the old city.

they count as one, despite the fact that they are clearly separate entities.

The fortified city – Cité de Caracssonne – is a UNESCO World Heritage Site. It has a double ring of massive ramparts with 53 towers. Medieval walls are built on Roman foundations, emphasizing the importance of Carcassonne in historical times, standing as it does in a gap between the Massif Central and the Pyrenees, where two roads cross (Atlantic to Mediterranean, Massif Central to Spain). It became an important trading centre that changed hands frequently by marriage or force of arms.

The UNESCO citation recognizes pioneering conservation work done in the 19th century by architect Eugène Viollet-le-Duc. The old city was scheduled for demolition, but saved after a local campaign and restored over many years, not altogether authentically. Even so, the effect is stunning. Only a few hundred people live there now, many of them traditional craftspeople. Just walk around, enjoying the walls, towers, 12th-century castle, Cathedral (Basilica-Saint-Nazarius, begun in the 11th century) and ancient streets.

The lower city (Ville Basse) across the River Aude was founded by King Louis IX in 1247, after Carcassonne submitted to French rule. This medieval city grew rich on the manufacture of shoes and textiles, declined in the 17th century and nowadays thrives on tourism – three million visitors arrive to see the old city each year, supplemented by those cruising the wonderful Canal du Midi (also a UNESCO World Heritage Site). The medieval heart of modern Carcassonne (Bastide Saint-Louis) is itself a delightful enclave centred on Place Carnot with its Fountain of Neptune (1770) and traditional market.

Paris

This global city sits astride the River Seine – whose banks are a UNESCO World Heritage Site – in the middle of a vast urban conurbation that is home to 12 million people, underlining the huge national and international significance of Paris.

As might be expected of the world's most popular tourist destination, Paris tests the superlatives with amazing architecture, incredible museums, world-class galleries, fabulous parks, great theatres, elegant boulevards, classy shops, gourmet restaurants, lively cafés . . . and the iconic Eiffel Tower.

Despite its relative youth, this has become the city's symbol, and those willing to climb 700-odd steps (and travel on by lift) see a stunning city panorama that has been enjoyed by over 200 million people since the tower opened in 1887. It is the tallest structure in Paris, though it lost the world title to New York's Chrysler Building in 1930.

Paris has a list of landmarks that goes on and on – Cathédrale-Notre-Dame (of Hunchback fame), Arc de Triomphe, Champs-Elysées, Sacré Coeur, Les Invalides, Panthéon, Opéra Garnier, Grande Arche . . . and many more. To those may be added museums like the Louvre, Musée National d'Art Moderne, Musée d'Orsay . . . and many more. Then there are famous quarters like the Rive Gauche, Faubourg Saint-Honairé, L'Opéra, Montmartre, Les Halles, Quartier Latin, Montparnasse . . . and many more.

Yes, it's overwhelming – but actually that doesn't matter. There's so much to see, do and enjoy that it would be impossible to cram everything into a lifetime, let alone one visit. So the answer is simple – go with the flow in the knowledge that wherever it takes you will provide a rewarding experience. Then promise to come back next year.

POPULATION:
2,200,000 (2006)

WHEN TO GO:
In the springtime, of course! However, canny crowd-haters know the city gets emptier for a month from 15 July for annual holidays.

DON'T MISS:
Leonardo Da Vinci's enigmatic *Mona Lisa* (*La Gioconda*) in the Louvre, if only to smile back personally at the world's most famous picture.
A stroll down Avenue Montaigne, to see the fabulous designer shops.
The foundation stone of modern France – Place de la Bastille where the infamous jail was stormed to mark the start of the French Revolution in 1789 (it only contained seven prisoners).
Parks like the Tuileries Gardens (created in the 16th century for a riverside palace) and the Luxembourg Gardens on the Left Bank (another former château garden).
The very heart of the ancient city – Île de la Cité, one of the city's two river islands, now home to important civic buildings as well as Notre-Dame.

YOU SHOULD KNOW:
Gustave Eiffel first offered his tower to Barcelona . . . but the Spanish city rejected it.

NEXT: *A view across the Seine to Notre Dame*

The Loire and its Châteaux

The term Loire Valley is usually used to refer to the area between Orléans and Angers. The valley effectively divides France – to the north the climate is mild and wet but to the south it abruptly changes to

WHEN TO GO:
Spring and autumn are the best times.
HIGHLIGHTS:
The Angers Tapestry, the Châteaux de Chambord, Chinon and Blois.
DON'T MISS:
Vineyards producing famous wines such as Sancerre and Muscadet.
YOU SHOULD KNOW:
The Loire Valley is often referred to as 'the Garden of France'.

The Château of Chambord

the drier, hotter climate of the Mediterranean. There is a wealth of history, art and architecture to be found here and it is also famous for its food and wines – Sancerre and Muscadet, Chinon and Bourgeuil to mention but a few. This is a wonderful place to explore and enjoy.

A spiral staircase at Château de Blois

It is an immensely fertile area, which – along with the easy transport provided by the river – made it highly desirable to wealthy lords and royalty, so the string of fabulous châteaux that can be seen today were built. There are so many of these gems that you could spend several weeks trying to visit them all. This is no doubt why UNESCO designated the whole area a World Heritage Site instead of attempting to pick out individual châteaux for that distinction.

Chenonceaux, built in 1520 by a tax collector for his wife, is often thought to be the most romantic of castles. Its design was always controlled by the women who lived here, including Diane de Poitiers and Catherine de Medici. Azay-le-Rideau is a classic fairy-tale palace with its white walls and early Renaissance style. It stands in lovely gardens on its own little island in the Indre River. The château at Villandry is renowned for its ornamental 'garden of love' and its wonderful kitchen garden. Fontevraud Abbey, which contains the tombs of the Plantagenets, is a superb complex of Romanesque buildings and the largest abbey in France.

Ile de Ré

Just 3 km (2 mi) off France's Atlantic coast, facing La Rochelle, lies the 30 km (19 mi) long Ile de Ré. It is an island of fine sandy beaches, whitewashed cottages, wild hollyhocks, salt marshes and it has a luminosity so delicate it begs to be photographed. Centuries of human activity, principally salt extraction, have shaped the land, turning what was four islands into one. Wine and oysters are now the island's mainstays, its vineyards belonging to the same appellation controlée as Cognac.

The Ile de Ré is one of the sunniest parts of France. Its climate is mild and the vegetation has an almost Mediterranean feel. Palm trees grow readily, and the contrast of white houses against the deep

Bicycles are the order of the day on the Ile de Ré.

POPULATION:
16,000 (winter), 160,000 (summer) (2004)

HOW TO GET THERE:
Across the toll bridge (near La Rochelle).

WHEN TO GO:
All year round but it can get very crowded in high summer.

HIGHLIGHTS:
The 15th century Eglise St-Martin – a fine Gothic church.
Hotel de Clerjotte – a naval and art museum.
The Ars-en-Ré Market – for a fine selection of local produce.
The Phare des Baleines – the views from the top of this lighthouse are stunning.
Lileau des Nigres – a maze of marshes and one of Europe's top bird-watching sites.

YOU SHOULD KNOW:
From the mid-19th century until World War II the citadel at St-Martin was used to house prisoners on their way to be transported to the colonies. Most met a swift end; one resident who didn't was Henri Charriére, aka Papillon, who managed to escape on a sack of coconuts after 13 years of enforced exile and later went on to write a bestseller about it.

blue sky evokes some Greek village adrift on the Atlantic. A toll bridge from the mainland was completed in 1987, which was to change the character of the island irrevocably. However even the heavy flow of summer visitors and second-homeowners has not been able to dent Ré's charm and in the winter the island is lived in and tranquil. Once across the bridge you have a choice of two routes. The north road goes to the pretty harbour of St-Martin-de-Ré; the south road leads you through farm villages and onto long

beaches. Eventually both roads merge, leading to the more rugged western cape of the island.

The island can easily be toured in a weekend, but you will need more time to explore the proper way, by bicycle. Long before the bridge brought carloads of tourists, Rétias, as the islanders are known, conducted their lives on bikes, and they still do. A remarkable system of narrow lanes connecting villages, vineyards and beaches takes you where cars can't.

Hollyhocks line a street in La Flotte.

51

Gorges du Tarn

The Gorges du Tarn have long been considered one
of the most beautiful sights in France. Over millions
of years, the River Tarn has found itself a route
through the limestone of the Grands Causses, slowly
eroding away the soft stone, forming steep cliffs

ry. Starting at Mont Lozère in
er runs some 370 km (230 mi)
ly direction before joining the
section through the Grands
he Causse du Larzac, for
a. This 60-km (37-mi) stretch is
pecially from the roads that
switch back and forth as
they climb up the high walls
of the valley. The aptly
named Point Sublime is one
of the best places to stop to
catch the views, and perhaps
to catch your breath.

A new attraction in the
area is the bridge across the
valley near Millau. Cars soar
270 m (885 ft) above the
river, giving the passengers a
view across the whole valley.

However, for those with
no head for heights or no
need for speed, there are
other ways to explore the
gorge: it is possible to take a
trip on a glass-bottomed boat
to watch the rocks drift past
beneath you, walk along the
riverside footpath or paddle
your way downstream by
canoe, looking out for the
owls and birds of prey that
play in the updraughts.
From this perspective, you
get a true sense of the scale
of this valley, which dwarves
the buildings and people
within it.

WHAT IS IT?
A spectacular gorge in
south-western France.
HOW TO GET THERE:
By road from Toulouse or
Montpellier.
WHEN TO GO:
Summer
NEAREST TOWN:
Millau
DON'T MISS:
The drive over the new
Millau viaduct.
YOU SHOULD KNOW:
The river can gain height
rapidly after heavy rains.

The Gorges du Tarn

Nice

This city on the French Riviera (Cote d'Azur) was founded by Greeks around 350 BC and changed hands many times before finally becoming part of France in 1860. Once the preserve of the rich and sometimes infamous, Nice has proved an enormous draw to incomers of many nationalities as well as a multitude of holidaymakers, making it a cosmopolitan place.

Despite some reminders of its long pre-tourist history, Nice is not a destination heritage lovers place top of their list, though the lively old town above the harbour is a picturesque maze of jumbled streets and alleys with many interesting houses. Other notable features include the Baroque Chapelle de la Miséricorde, the 17th-century Cathedral with its unusual bell tower and the quirky Italianate Liscaris Palace.

No, the true *raison d'être* of Nice is simple – to offer people the pleasurable chance to experience a spicy Mediterranean resort. Before wading in, two 'do nots' are worth mentioning – don't expect to enjoy the Nice experience on the cheap (everything's expensive) and don't expect to find any sandy beaches (there are none). The city does have a wonderful touch of sophistication, though, with grand hotels, classic 19th-century villas, garden squares with fountains, the famous Promenade des Anglais running along the horseshoe of the Baie des Anges, terraced cafés and classy restaurants. But it definitely isn't as exclusive as it once was.

For those with cultural leanings, Nice has plentiful offerings. The Musée Chagall has stained glass by the famous artist. There is a Matisse Museum and the Musée des Beaux-Arts, with the original plaster cast of Rodin's *The Kiss*. The Museum of Modern and Contemporary Art near the bus station is housed in a suitably dramatic set of four connected towers. Then it's back to the seafront!

POPULATION:
347,000 (2006)
WHEN TO GO:
Any time except mid-July to mid-August, when the town is very hot and extremely crowded.
DON'T MISS:
The view from the ruined castle overlooking the harbour – it's a stiff climb, but worth the effort.
A busy daily market on Cours Saleya selling fresh produce and a great selection of flowers (antiques on Mondays).
The Cathedral of St Nicholas – an impressive Russian orthodox church built in 1859, now a French national monument.
The hilltop quarter of Cimiez that is definitely the classiest area in Nice.
Local speciality pissaladière – a savoury tart with onions, anchovies and olives.
An ice cream or 70 (that's how many flavours there are) from the famous Glacier Fenocchio opposite the Cathedral.
YOU SHOULD KNOW:
That huge yellow villa on the top of Mount Alban belongs to singer Elton John.

The old harbour

Heidelberg

There was a time when it was de rigueur amongst the German aristocracy to have a duelling scar on the cheek, earned in single combat at Heidelberg's ancient university. Even now, looking across the River Neckar

past the glorious Old Bridge (18th century) to the castle on the wooded hills of Odenwald (Odin's Forest) beyond, one might still be in that vanished era.

In fact, Heidelberg owes its historic character to the fact that it wasn't bombed in World War II, because the Americans had earmarked this city in the south west of

The old bridge and castle in Heidelberg

*Karlsplatz in
Heidelberg*

POPULATION:
145,000 (2008)
WHEN TO GO:
For something different, try
December for a traditional
German Christmas Market,
held throughout the old
town.
DON'T MISS:
A grim reminder of
Heidelberg's inglorious Nazi
past – the Thingstätte
amphitheatre built on the
Heiligenberg Mountain for
SS rallies (wonderful view
of the old town!).
The small Vetter's Brewery
near the Old Bridge, said to
brew one of the world's
strongest beers.
The apparently endless
Hauptstrasse (High Street) –
a shopper's paradise if ever
there was one.
University Square
(Universitätsplatz), to soak
up the atmosphere of the
medieval university
(founded here in 1386).
The Kurpfälzisches Museum
on Hauptstrasse, containing
exhibits from the city's pre-
history right up to modern
times.
YOU SHOULD KNOW:
The earliest known
European prehistoric man
lived here 500,000 years
ago – appropriately named
Heidelberg Man (jawbone
found nearby in 1907).

Germany as a desirable base when hostilities ceased
(they still have a military presence in and around the
city today). Since the war, the city has developed
rapidly, spreading out from the old centre, but it is the
old town that everyone wants to see.

It crouches along the river bank, beneath the not-to-
be-missed castle (started in the 14th century, added to
periodically until its abandonment in the 17th century).
Old Heidelberg has a Baroque charm all its own with
narrow streets and picturesque houses. Look out for
Karlstor, a triumphal gate completed in 1781, the fine
Heiliggeistkirche (Cathedral) and very old Zum Ritter
Sankt Georg (House of the Knight of St George). Since
the 18th century, Heidelberg has enjoyed a cultural
reputation as the centre of German Romanticism. Across
the river is Philosophers' Walk, where Heidelberg's
thinkers and university lecturers once walked and
talked, gazing at the romantic Schloss Heidelberg on
Königstuhl (King's Throne Hill) as they did so.

Heidelberg's economy is now based on the university
and tourism, the latter exploiting the city's rich heritage
to attract millions of visitors each year. To support this
activity, there are numerous festivals, frequent firework
displays, musical performances and markets . . . even a
half marathon.

Neuschwanstein

Built on a 92-m (300-ft) hill, Neuschwanstein, the royal palace in the Bavarian Alps of Germany, is the most famous of the three royal palaces built for Louis II of Bavaria, sometimes referred to as 'Mad King Ludwig'.

Named after the Swan Knight of Wagner's opera *Lohengrin*, the castle was exquisitely designed by Christian Jank. Located near the Hohenschwangau, where Ludwig was brought up in south-western Bavaria near the Austrian border, the enormous and whimsical castle is so spectacular that it inspired Walt Disney to use it as a model for Cinderella's castle, used on the Disney logo.

Ludwig was removed from power before the completion of the castle, which was opened to the public after his mysterious death in 1886. An embodiment of nineteenth-century Romanticism, the castle is reached by a meandering road that leads from the valley to the front gate.

After 17 years' work, only 14 of the 360 rooms were finished before Ludwig's death, but these alone are worth the trip. The Throne Room was designed in elaborate Byzantine style as the Grail-Hall of Parsifal. Inspired by the Aya Sophia in Istanbul, the two-storey throne room has a series of pillars made of imitation porphyry and lapis lazuli.

Ludwig's obsession with the legends on which Wagner based his operas continues in the other rooms: *Tannhauser* in the study, grotto and conservatory, *Lohengrin* in the salon and study, the *Nibelungenlied* in the dining room and lower hall and the *Meistersinger von Nürnberg* in the dressing room. The bedroom features paintings of scenes from *Tristan and Isolde*. The Singers Hall is also decorated with episodes from *Parsifal*.

But Neuschwanstein is about more than one man's obsession with his medieval ancestors, it is a beautiful, visionary place, which sits perfectly within the stunning landscape of the Bavarian Alps.

WHAT IS IT?
A nineteenth-century castle in the Bavarian Alps and one of Germany's most popular tourist destinations.
WHERE IS IT:
South-west Bavaria near the Austrian border.
HIGHLIGHTS:
The whimsical castle that inspired the Disney Castle.
YOU SHOULD KNOW:
The 1968 film *Chitty Chitty Bang Bang* was partly filmed here.

NEXT:
Neuschwanstein Castle

The Rhine Valley

The Middle Rhine Valley in western Germany, with its castles, historic towns and vineyards, has a dramatic and varied natural landscape, a natural timeline of the area's historical and cultural past and sheer, majestic beauty of its own.

A UNESCO World Heritage Site since 2002, the Upper Middle Rhine Valley (Oberes Mittelrheintal) is both beautiful and an outstanding example of how its role as one of the most important transport routes in Europe for thousands of years facilitated cultural exchange between the Mediterranean and the north.

The steep slopes of the river have been terraced for agriculture for hundreds of years, and the warm south-facing slopes make ideal areas for the cultivation of grapes for the region's famous wines and add to the beauty of the river valley.

The captivating views of the narrow valley, dotted with pretty towns and ruined castles and surrounded by towering mountains have made this one of Germany's most important areas for tourism. Its waters are plied by both commercial and pleasure craft, especially cruisers, and the banks are home to more than 20 castles and historic ruins. Only two of the many fortresses, Pfalzgrafenstein near Kaub-in-the-Rhine, and the Marksburg by Braubach, are well preserved, most of the rest of the historic buildings, such as the Werner Kapelle and the Chapel in Bacharach, were ruined long ago, while others have been converted into hotels.

One of the best-known attractions in the river, which is seen to advantage from a boat cruise, is the Lorelei rock near St Goarshausen. It rises 120 m (390 ft) above the water, and there are many legends about the water spirit who is said to lure men to their doom here.

Since the Age of Enlightenment, the remarkable

Burg Stahleck, Bacharach

Altes Haus, Bacharach

beauty of the Middle Rhine has captured the imagination of musicians, artists and writers. The romantic visions of the crumbling feudal castles, the lush emerald valleys and the dramatic mountains have inspired poets, authors and composers such as Lord Byron, Alexandre Dumas, Victor Hugo and Richard Wagner.

Lübeck

Situated on the Trave River in Schleswig-Holstein, northern Germany, Lübeck is the largest German port on the Baltic Sea. Its old town is a charming collection of well-preserved churches, merchants' homes, narrow alleyways and warehouses that have been designated by UNESCO as a World Heritage Site.

In the fourteenth century, Lübeck was the 'Queen of the Hanseatic League', the largest and most powerful member of the trade alliance which operated a monopoly over the Baltic Sea and much of Europe. In 1375, Emperor Charles IV named Lübeck one of the five 'Glories of the Empire'; the other four being Venice, Rome, Pisa and Florence.

The old town, in the heart of the city, is dominated by church steeples, including that of the Cathedral (Lübecker Dom). Started in 1173 by Henry the Lion as a cathedral for the Bishop of Lübeck, it was partly destroyed by bombing in World War II but later reconstructed. Constructed from 1250 to 1350, St Mary's (Marienkirche) is also a dominant presence in the old town. It is the third largest church in Germany, and the tallest building in the old part of Lübeck.

Lubeck's old town also boasts an impressive Town Hall (Rathaus), still in use, and the Art Nouveau Stadttheater, the Heiligen-Geist-Hospital and the Schiffergesellschaft can also be found here. The narrow lanes and alleyways of Lübeck's old town are lined with Gothic, Renaissance, Baroque and Classical town houses with red-brick, gabled façades. There is a multitude of interesting museums, with themes including the history of art, ethnology, fine art, the history of the city, theatre puppets and nature and the environment. One of the best ways to enjoy this lovely city is to take a boat trip around the harbour, leaving from the Holsten Bridge.

POPULATION:
213,000 (2005)
WHEN TO GO:
May to October
DON'T MISS:
Lübecker Dom – started in 1173 by Henry the Lion and completed in 1230. The Eastern Vault was destroyed on Palm Sunday 1942 by a bombing raid.
Marienkirche – the tallest church in the city, was completed by 1350 and was seen as a symbol of power and prosperity.
The Stadttheater, a listed Art Noveau playhouse.
A stroll in the old town, which is home to over 1,000 listed buildings.
A boat trip along the Trave Canal – take in old city fortresses, mills, the medieval city walls before passing the scenic 'Painter's Corner' and Holsten Gate.
YOU SHOULD KNOW:
Lübeck is famous for its marzipan.

NEXT: St Marien and St Petri cathedral towers

Amsterdam

POPULATION:
760,000 (2009)
WHEN TO GO:
Between May and
September
DON'T MISS:
Boat tour of the canals – a
great way to see the city's
best sights.
Oude Kerk – the oldest
church in Amsterdam. The
roof is the largest medieval
wooden vault in Europe.
Anne Frank House on the
Prinsengracht – the former
hiding place where Anne
wrote her famous diary tells
the history of the eight
people who were in hiding
here. Her diary is among the
original objects
on display.
Van Gogh Museum –
exhibits the largest
collection of his paintings in
the world.
The nightlife – Amsterdam
is one of Europe's premier
party cities and offers
something for every taste!
YOU SHOULD KNOW:
The city has an amazing
diversity of cultural and
historical attractions.

Amsterdam started out in the 13th century as a small
fishing village. According to legend, it was founded by
two Frisian fishermen, who landed on the shores of
the Amstel river in a small boat with their dog. The
damming of the river gave the village its name. Today

it is the capital of the Netherlands, known for its liberal attitudes, rich culture and history. The city has kilometres of attractive canals, some truly great art collections, stunning architecture and many fascinating museums.

Few early buildings survive, except the medieval Oude Kerk (the Old Church, with little houses on its

The Prinsengracht is best explored by boat.

sides), the Neuwe Kerk (New Church) and the Houten Huis (Wooden House). The historical centre was largely built during the Golden Age in the 17th century, when Amsterdam was one of the wealthiest cities in the world, with trade links to the Baltic, North America, Africa, Indonesia and Brazil. Its stock exchange was the first to trade continuously. This period saw the building of the classical Royal Palace on Damplein, the Westerkerk, Zuiderkerk, and many canal houses, including De Dolfijn (Dolphin) and De Gecroonde Raep (the Crowned Turnip).

Amsterdam has many outstanding museums, including the Rijksmuseum, the Stedelijk Museum and the Rembrandt House Museum. The Van Gogh Museum houses the largest collection of the artist's work in the world. Anne Frank House on the Prinsengracht is where the Jewish diarist hid during World War II to avoid Nazi persecution, and is well worth a visit.

Amsterdam is famous for its canals. The three main canals extend from the IJ Lake, and each of these marks the position of the city

The city's canal houses look stunning by night.

Houseboats line the canals.

walls and moat at different periods in time. The innermost is the Herengracht (Lord's Canal). Beyond it lie the Keizersgracht (Emperor's Canal) and the Prinsengracht (Prince's Canal). They are best enjoyed by boat, or by bicycle along the surrounding streets. Smaller canals intersect the main canals, dividing the city into a number of islands, and nearly 1,300 bridges criss-cross the waterways of this beautiful city, known as the 'Venice of the North'.

Amsterdam is also known for its nightlife, with its bustling cafés, restaurants, clubs, traditional 'brown' bars, cinemas and theatres. These are mainly centred around the Leidseplein, the Jordaan and Rembrandtplein. Many visitors go for the infamous Red Light District, with its legalized prostitution, strip joints and sex shops.

Oxford

Described as the 'city of dreaming spires' by Matthew Arnold, the nineteenth-century English poet and cultural critic, in reference to its harmonious college buildings, Oxford is home to the oldest university in the English-speaking world. It stands at the meeting

POPULATION:
153,000 (2008)
WHEN TO GO:
In summer for punting on the river.
DON'T MISS:
Magdelen College
Balliol College
Christ Church
Radcliffe Camera – the circular dome and drum is one of the city's most distinctive landmarks. The camera (which simply means 'room') was built in 1737 by the royal physician Dr John Radcliffe.
The Sheldonian Theatre
The Pitt Rivers Museum
YOU SHOULD KNOW:
Most colleges have opening hours for visitors and entry fees.

The dome of the Radcliffe Camera, part of the Bodleian Library and the quad of All Souls college in the evening light

point of two rivers: the Cherwell and the Isis, as the Thames is known at this point. The city dates back to Saxon times, but it was not until the twelfth century that its Augustinian abbey began to take and educate students. A century later, the first colleges were founded; others followed as the student population grew.

Most tourists come to Oxford to see the colleges. Among the best are Magdalen College with its beautiful grounds and the distinctive Magdalen Tower, and Christ Church, a grand collection of buildings around an enormous courtyard founded by Cardinal Thomas Woolsey, with its tower built by Sir Christopher Wren.

Oxford also boasts some of the best-known museums in the world. The Ashmolean Museum of Art and Archaeology is noted for its collections of Pre-Raphaelite paintings, Majolica pottery and English silver. The archaeology department has an excellent collection of Greek and Minoan pottery, and some important antiquities from Ancient Egypt. The Pitt Rivers Museum is also world famous, with its wonderful archaeological and anthropological collections.

The circular dome and drum of the Radcliffe Camera is one of the most distinctive landmarks in Oxford. Built in the eighteenth century to house a new library, the Camera is today used as the main reading room of the Bodleian Library. The Sheldonian Theatre also warrants a visit. Built in 1667, it was the first major commission for Christopher Wren. Then Professor of Astronomy at Oxford, Wren designed the Sheldonian to imitate a classical Roman theatre.

As well as its dreaming spires, Oxford is known for its rivers. These offer beautiful riverbank walks and the opportunity to hire a punt and spend a lazy afternoon messing about on the river.

*The quad of
Jesus College*

Bath

The City of Bath is founded around the only naturally occurring hot springs in the United Kingdom. It was first documented as a Roman spa in around 43 AD, although tradition suggests that it was founded earlier. The waters from its spring were believed to have medicinal properties. During the Roman period increasingly grand temples and bathing complexes were built around the springs, including the Great Bath. Rediscovered gradually from the eighteenth century onwards, they have become one of the city's main attractions. The Roman Baths Museum gives a fascinating insight into the Roman complex that was here – you can see the ruins of the 2,000 year old temple or drink the waters in the Pump Room. Part of the complex has recently been refurbished to provide a modern spa.

In the tenth century a monastery was founded at Bath, but the Abbey as it is today was not built until the sixteenth century. Medieval Bath was a prosperous wool-trading town, but it was not until the eighteenth century that Bath became the leading centre of fashionable life in England. It was during this time that Bath's Theatre Royal was built, as well as architectural triumphs such as the Royal Crescent, Lansdown Crescent, the Circus and Pulteney Bridge. Master of Ceremonies Beau Nash, who presided over the city's social life from 1705 until his death in 1761, drew up a code of behaviour for public entertainments.

Today Bath is known for its Georgian architectural gems which are still beautifully preserved. The Royal Crescent is a magnificent curve of Georgian houses built between 1767 and 1775, only a short walk from the Circus, a circle of 30 beautiful town houses. Many famous people have lived here, including David Livingstone and Clive of India.

POPULATION:
90,000 (2006)
WHEN TO GO:
Any time of year.
DON'T MISS:
The Roman Baths
Museum of Costume
The Assembly Rooms
The Royal Crescent
Jane Austen Centre
Castle Combe
Lacock Abbey
YOU SHOULD KNOW:
The city is a UNESCO World Heritage Site.

NEXT: People play a fun game of cricket on the lawns in front of the Royal Crescent. Designed by John Wood the Younger between 1728-1801, the Royal Crescent is one of Bath's most impressive buildings.

The Lake District

Lying in the north-west of England, the Lake District is one of the best-loved landscapes in the country and has been celebrated in poetry and literature – from Wordsworth's *Daffodils* to Ransome's *Swallows*

WHAT IS IT?
An area of outstanding beauty and a national park in north-western England.
HOW TO GET THERE:
By road, or by rail to Windermere.
WHEN TO GO:
Any time
NEAREST TOWN:
Kendal 10 km (6 mi).
YOU SHOULD KNOW:
The weather in the high fells is often worse than at lower levels, so be prepared.

A paddle steamer on Ullswater

and Amazons – and art. It is the highest area in England, and its fells are wonderful hiking territory. The U-shaped valleys that radiate out from the centre of the area were carved out of the rock by glaciers during the last ice age. Where the underlying rock is soft, the valleys and hills are

gentle, but in the middle where the rocks are volcanic the skyline is full of jagged edges where the grinding ice ripped rocks apart.

The higher fells, like Scafell Pike, Helvellyn, Skiddaw and Great Gable are challenging hikes and not for the beginner, but the softer areas near Windermere itself are easier.

Windermere is the largest lake in England, and Wast Water the deepest. Windermere, Derwentwater and Coniston Water are popular for boating, and can get busy, but the more remote lakes are far more peaceful. Higher up are smaller tarns that sit in glacial cirques.

The Lake District is not large, only 56 km (35 mi) across at its widest, but its sheer variety of scenery – from rolling hills to rugged moorland and bare jagged rock and from peaceful lakes to rushing mountain streams – and the continually changing light as clouds rush across the landscape make this area so dramatic and very beautiful.

The sun sets over Derwentwater.

Sark

Sark is the smallest of the four main Channel Islands. It lies in the English Channel, about 128 km (80 mi) from England and about 32 km (20 mi) from the coast of Normandy. It is as well that it is small, as there are no cars on the island, and transport other than on foot consists of horse-drawn carriages, tractors and bicycles.

Sark's history is long, and complex. Until the mid 16th century it was a place of pirates, frequently invaded by the French. In 1563, Helier de Carteret, the Seigneur of St Ouen in Jersey, received a charter from Elizabeth I to settle on Sark. After nearly 450 years, Sark's feudal parliament, known as the Chief Pleas, and mainly comprising unelected island landowners, was scrapped by Britain's Privy Council. In December 2008, the people of Sark elected 28 Conseillers to the Island's parliament.

The backdrop to this newfound democracy is comprised of steep, rocky cliffs, gorgeous sandy beaches and coves, and woods filled with springtime bluebells. Over 600 different plants and wildflowers grow here. Seabirds nest on the cliffs, and birds of prey, songbirds and migrants enjoy its stunning unspoilt landscape.

Greater Sark is connected to Little Sark by a narrow, paved isthmus known as La Coupée. Just 2.7 m (9 ft) wide, it has dizzying 90 m (300 ft) drops to either side. La Seigneurie, de Carteret's manor house built in 1565, is believed to stand on the site of an early Christian monastery. Although privately owned, its gardens, some of the finest in the Channel Islands, are open to the public.

POPULATION:
610 (2002)
WHEN TO GO:
Any time, but April to October may provide the best weather.
HOW TO GET THERE:
By ferry from Guernsey, Jersey and Normandy.
HIGHLIGHTS:
St Peter's Church (1820).
Sark Prison – built in 1856 and capable of accommodating only two people, this is the smallest prison in the world.
La Grande Greve, perhaps Sark's most special bay.
A walk through Dixcart valley to the ancient cannon at Hogs Back.
The Boutique and Gouliot Caves.
Swimming at low tide in the Venus Pool on Little Sark.

NEXT: La Coupée, the isthmus connecting Little Sark to Big Sark.

The Scottish Lochs

There are hundreds of stunning lochs splashed like raindrops all over Scotland and exploring them all could take a lifetime – this is some of the most beautiful landscape in the British Isles. The lochs were formed during the last Ice Age, which sculpted this dramatic landscape in combination with ancient volcanic activity. Loch Lomond is the largest and contains the greatest area of fresh water in the British Isles. Its shores are lined with native oakwoods and its waters are home to 17 native species of fish. Loch Lomond is the centrepiece of the Loch Lomond and Trossachs National Park. It is 39 km (24 mi) long and incredibly beautiful. However, as it is so easily accessible from Glasgow, it is often very busy.

To the west of Loch Lomond, on the far side of the Cowal Peninsula, lies the sea loch Loch Fyne, which is renowned for its oysters and its sea fishing. A short distance north of the head of the loch is the Bentmore Botanic Garden. Affiliated with Edinburgh's Royal Botanic Garden it is particularly famous for its wonderful show of rhododendrons in the late spring.

The strikingly beautiful Eilean Donan Castle in the North West Highlands is also well worth a visit. It is majestically situated on an island at the point where three great sea lochs meet and has become an iconic image of Scotland.

WHAT IS IT?
The lochs of Scotland provide some of the most beautiful scenery in the country and are scattered around the Highlands of Scotland.

HIGHLIGHTS:
Whether you like fishing, sailing or enjoying freshly caught, local food there is something for everyone in this beautiful setting.

DON'T MISS:
Urquhart, Loch Leven and Eilean Donan castles, Culloden Moor, the Loch Ness monster!

YOU SHOULD KNOW:
Eilean Donan has featured in a number of films and television programmes ranging from *Elizabeth – The Golden Age* and *Made of Honour* to *Rob Roy* and *Highlander.*

Eilean Donan Castle

Skye

No doubt the best known of all the Scottish islands, Skye, which is about 80 km (50 mi) from top to bottom, has a great many things going for it, not least the most achingly beautiful scenery. Ever since the Victorians discovered the joys of climbing the spectacular Cuillin Ridge, the island has attracted more and more tourists, and this, in the summer months, together with its notoriously changeable climate, is its only downside.

Visited by St Columba in 585 AD, Skye was in the hands of the Norsemen for 300 years before being divided by three Scots clans, who fought over it constantly. Its most famous resident, Flora MacDonald, achieved lasting fame for her help in the escape to France of Bonnie Prince Charlie in 1745, and her grave can be visited at Kilmuir. During the 1800s many families were forced to leave the island due to the

disastrous Jacobite rebellion and the clearances. Today, tourism is the backbone of the economy, and a bridge has been built to link the island to the mainland.

The biggest draw is the Cuillin Ridge, which is a fantastic area for climbing and hill-walking, but the northern Trotternish Peninsula is equally inspiring, with amazing coastal views and weird and wonderful rock formations such as Kilt Rock and the 50-m (165-ft) high rock needle, the Old Man of Storr. This last is only a few miles from Skye's main town, Portree – a pretty little place on a deep sea loch.

On the west coast, the Minginish Peninsula is worthy of a visit. If the weather is inclement, or you have had enough walking, drop into the famous Talisker Distillery. Founded in 1830, its single malt whisky was a favourite of Robert Louis Stevenson, and since then it has become the favourite of a great many more people too!

The view from The Quirang to Trotternish Ridge on the Trotternish Peninsula

Segovia

The historic heart of Segovia is a UNESCO World Heritage Site, and it is easy to see why. This compact hill-top city is old Spain and Castille at its very best, with narrow pedestrian streets, intriguing alleys rich with the aromas of regional cooking and Europe's highest concentration of Romanesque churches.

A chateau in Segovia is the perfect place to soak up the atmosphere of historic Spain.

Around it all is a city wall with towers and gates, bordered by two rivers and a girdle of trees offering peaceful, shaded walks. And that's before mentioning the impressive Alcázar castle and famous aqueduct.

This is a place to soak up the atmosphere of historic Spain. The elongated Alcázar, rising from its rocky crag above the city and looking almost like a giant stone ship, sits on Roman and Moorish foundations. It was built, extended, altered and restored over many centuries of use successively as royal residence, prison and artillery school. Nowadays, it is one of the most popular historical sights in Spain.

Another is the astonishing double-arched Roman aqueduct, rising to a height of 28.5 m (93.5 ft) in the pedestrianised Azoguejo Square, where it is at its most impressive – though this is but the climax to an ingenious irrigation system stretching into the mountains that still carries water today.

Segovia has wonderful churches. The late-Gothic Cathedral with its dominant tower stands at the city's highest point, and has a richly decorated interior. The Church of St Martin is surrounded by a beautiful atrium and has a 12th century marble relief of its saint. San Juan de los Caballeros with its striking interior carving was the church of choice for Segovia's noble families.

Luckily, there are dozens of pavement cafés, restaurants and interesting shops for those who need a break from sightseeing, which can be quite exhausting in this most enchanting of cities.

POPULATION:
56,000 (2004)
WHEN TO GO:
Summer, when the temperature is ideal thanks to the city's mountainous setting.
DON'T MISS:
The extraordinary 15th century House of Points, covered with pointed studs, causing it to change appearance as the sun moves.
Lozoya's Tower, a 14th century defensive structure, beside a statue of Juan Bravo by renowned sculptor Aniceto Marinas, celebrating the defeat of a peasants' revolt.
The Monastery of San Antonio, outside the city – once a royal hunting lodge, then a monastery, with an exquisite interior.
The circular Church of Veracruz, across the River Eresma, founded by the Knights Templar in the 12th century.
The ancient quarter of Canonigos, centred on the 13th century St Stephen's Church with its magnificent tower.
The carving attributed to 17th century Florentine artist Gregorio Fernandez in St Andrew's Church.
YOU SHOULD KNOW:
Segovia's historic 16th century mint is the world's oldest extant industrial manufactory.

NEXT: The skyline of Segovia, dominated by the cathedral

89

Granada

This distinctive city at the foot of the Sierra Nevada
Mountains has been a settlement since the dawn of

time, but it is forever associated with the period when it was under Moorish rule (8th to 15th centuries, in 1492 it became the last enclave to be retaken by the Catholic Spanish monarchy). The reason may be summarized in two words – the Alhambra. This

The Alhambra Palace dominates the area below the Sierra Nevada mountains.

POPULATION:
237,000 (2007)
WHEN TO GO:
Spring and autumn when
the days are warm and
sunny, and the temperature
is perfect.
DON'T MISS:
Sacromonte, a hill
overlooking the city from
the north, where Granada's
large gypsy community
once inhabited cave
dwellings and now a centre
for traditional flamenco
dancing.
The Bib-Rambla quarter for
an open-air meal, before
exploring the narrow street
of the Arab bazaar that
runs to the Cathedral.
Granada Cathedral itself,
Spain's finest Renaissance-
style church – started in
1529, continued for nearly
200 years and never
completed (no spires!).
The Charterhouse, a
Carthusian monastery
founded in 1506 – a fine
example of Spanish
Baroque architecture, with
an extensive picture
collection on view.
The 8th/9th century
Bermejas Towers – strong
points on the walls
surrounding the Alhambra.
The Archaeological
Museum of Granada in
Castril Palace, in the old
Arab area of Ajsaris
favoured by the city's
Renaissance grandees.
YOU SHOULD KNOW:
The city's first bishop and
patron saint, Cecilio, is said
to have been martyred in
the ancient catacombs
under Sacromonte Abbey.

amazing hilltop palace and fortress complex above
the city, begun in the 13th century, tells the story
of Moorish presence in southern Spain – arriving
as warlike conquerers and departing as sophisticated
aesthetes. The Alhambra is stunning – though
constantly altered and abused in subsequent
centuries, it remains an awe-inspiring monument to
the distinctive local brand of Islamic culture and
craftsmanship that reached incomparable heights
in Granada.

The Alhambra shares the distinction of being a
UNESCO World Heritage Site with two more
wonderful legacies of the long-lasting Moorish
presence – the nearby Palace of Generalife (summer
residence of the Moorish rulers) and the old casbah of
Albaicín, a maze of narrow streets with whitewashed
houses and a wonderful view of the Alhambra on the
facing hill from St Salvador's Church which – like so
many in the city – is built on the site of an earlier
mosque. Granada has the largest extant collection of
Moorish buildings in Europe, and parts of those that
have gone were frequently incorporated into
structures that replaced them and are still obvious
today. Even the *acequias* that feed the Arab
fountains, wells and baths are original.

A large student population ensures that Granada is
a lively place by day and night, with plenty of cafés,
bars and clubs – but paradoxically the Moorish capital
of southern Spain is quieter in the holidays when they
all go home.

*Intricate Moorish designs
decorate the palace – such
craftsmanship!*

If blue sky, blue sea, golden sand and a peaceful atmosphere is what you want, then Formentera is for you.

Formentera

Less than 6 km (4 miles) south of the party island of Ibiza, Formentera is its complete antithesis – an island with very little coastal development, and not a club in sight. Its relative inaccessibility and lack of water has protected it from the ravages of tourism and it is one of the least spoilt spots in the Mediterranean with only one proper tourist resort, Es Pujols.

The smallest and southernmost of the Balearics, as well as the hottest and driest, Formentera is famous for its peaceful, laid-back atmosphere and incredible stretches of white sand beach, often deserted, where nobody turns a hair at nudity. The scenery is dramatic – an arid, windswept landscape, wild and wooded, with a varied, indented 80 km (50 mi) long coastline which includes dunes, salt flats and innumerable sandy coves. The 19 km (12 mi) long, relatively flat island is best explored by bike. Country lanes lead past *fincas* (farmhouses) festooned with bougainvillea, stone-walled vineyards, and small pastures where sheep and goats shelter in the shade of contorted fig trees. Wherever you are, the sea air is heady with the scent of rosemary, wild thyme, juniper and pine.

Life has always been hard on Formentera. Although there are signs of human habitation from more than 4,000 years ago, it was deserted for nearly 300 years between the early 16th and late 18th centuries for fear of pirates, until a few resourceful farmers resettled here, determined to eke out a living despite the lack of water. The island's fortune changed dramatically in the 1960s when hippies who had had their fill of Ibiza started to move here. It only took Bob Dylan to stay in a windmill on the island for it to acquire a reputation as the hippest spot in Europe – a reputation that has stuck fast and still stands today.

POPULATION:
7,461 (2002)

WHEN TO GO:
May to September for the perfect dream Mediterranean holiday experience.

HOW TO GET THERE:
A high-speed ferry departs from Ibiza approximately every hour.

HIGHLIGHTS:
The Blue Bar – one of the best beach cafés in the Balearics, in the middle of the famous Platja de Migjorn, a beautiful 5 km (3 mi) stretch of beach that runs along the south coast.
Faro de La Mola – a lighthouse standing on the highest point of the island, described by Jules Verne as a magical place in his novel *Hector Servadac*. The nearby town of El Pilar de la Mola has a beautiful church and Sunday hippie market.
Es Cap de Barbaria – walk along the cape to the lighthouse to watch the sun go down.
Estany des Peix – a lagoon with a narrow opening to the sea.

YOU SHOULD KNOW:
The strip of water between Formentera and Ibiza is a marine reserve dotted with islets, part of which is a UNESCO World Heritage Site. In order to dive in the reserve area, you must obtain a permit.

Lisbon

POPULATION:
600,000 (2006)
WHEN TO GO:
March to June
DON'T MISS:
The National Museum of
Ancient Art – located in a
17th-century palace, this is
one of Portugal's most
important museums due to
its collection of fine art,
sculpture, engravings,
jewellery, ceramics, textiles
and furniture.
The Museum Calouste
Gulbenkian.
The Jerónimos Monastery –
a vast homage to the
seafaring men who made
Portugal's name and a
textbook example of
Manueline architecture.
The Belem Tower – built as
a fortress in the middle of
the River Tagus to protect
Lisbon, though due to the
receding river it now stands
on almost dry ground.
The panoramic views of the
city from Castello de São
Jorge.
The church of São Roque.
YOU SHOULD KNOW:
There are entrance fees for
museums.

On the Atlantic coast where the River Tagus flows
into the ocean, lies Portugal's capital city of Lisbon
(Lisboa), nestled between seven hills. Lisbon is a
beautiful, relaxed city full of contrasts, from modern
high rises to Art Nouveau buildings, wonderful mosaic
pavements, brightly tiled buildings and medieval
Moorish architecture.

Its port has been in constant use for the last three
thousand years by a number of different rulers, but it
was most prominent and powerful between the
fifteenth and seventeenth centuries, when Portugal
was a wealthy nation. Much of this wealth was due to
the explorer Vasco da Gama, who discovered the sea

route to India in 1498. This led to a lively trade in spices and gem stones, bringing great wealth to Lisbon. In the seventeenth century, gold was discovered in Brazil, bringing in more money. However, in 1755 the city was severely damaged by an earthquake and the tsunami that followed. It was never to regain its former prominence.

Close to the harbour is the Praça do Comercio, one of the most elegant city squares in Europe. The surrounding buildings have attractive arcades along their facades. The city centre of Lisbon, Baixa, is organized in a grid pattern and was largely built after the earthquake. The oldest district is Alfama, close to the Tagus, which survived almost intact and retains many medieval buildings. For a view over the city,

Lisbon's skyline at dusk with two of its iconic monuments near the River Tagus – the Bridge of 25th April and the Holy Christ monument.

visit the Castello de São Jorge, a medieval castle built on a hill in the fortified citadel. The castle was the last stronghold of resistance if attackers managed to enter the citadel. It is a handsome rectangular building with ten towers.

Don't miss the façade of the church of Nossa Senhora da Conceição Velha. The church was rebuilt after the earthquake using rescued elements of the old building, mainly decorative pieces of the façade which date back to the sixteenth century. This façade is a great example of the Manueline style, or Portuguese Late Gothic, a sumptuous architectural style incorporating maritime elements and inspired by the discoveries of Vasco da Gama. This style marks the transition from Late Gothic to Renaissance.

Probably the most prominent monument of Lisbon and certainly the most successful achievement of the Manueline style is the magnificent Jerónimos Monastery, with its delightful cloister. Close by is the Belem Tower, built in the early sixteenth century to commemorate Vasco da Gama. This defensive, yet elegant construction is one of the symbols of the city, a memorial to Portugal's power during the Age of the Great Discoveries.

Musicians playing Fado music in bar.

Venice

Gondolas near the Rialto Bridge

Once the wealthiest city in Europe, Venice is arguably also the most beautiful. Built on wooden piles in the middle of a lagoon on Italy's Adriatic coast, Venice wears its riches with pride. In its heyday, this city state had strong trade links with the Byzantine Empire and the Muslim world. During the late thirteenth century, over 3,300 Venetian trade ships dominated Mediterranean commerce. Throughout this prosperous time, the city's most prominent families competed with each other to build the grandest palaces and support the most talented artists.

The main artery of the city, the Grand Canal, sweeps in an elegant curve through its centre. A vaporetto (water-bus) trip down the Grand Canal will reveal the faded elegance of more than 300 palaces, illustrating the city's beautiful blend of Europe and Byzantium. And it is these private palaces and

POPULATION:
271,000 (2006)
WHEN TO GO:
The two weeks before Lent for the Carnevale.
DON'T MISS:
Murano – this island just north of Venice is famous for its glasswork.
A gondola ride.
Torcello – the most intriguing and atmospheric of the islands in the Venetian lagoon. Don't miss the stunning Basilica di Santa Maria Assunta on the dusty piazza.
The Lido – Venice's seaside.
La Fenice opera house, one of the most beautiful in the world.
YOU SHOULD KNOW:
The city is a UNESCO World Heritage Site.

houses, rather than the public monuments, which make Venice so appealing. Explored by gondola or on foot, the narrow alleys and backwaters of the city reveal all its decorative detail which reflects its past wealth and importance.

Venice was governed by the Great Council, made up of members of the most influential families. The Great Council appointed public officials and elected a Senate of 2–300 men. The Senate chose the Council of Ten, an elect group which handled the administration of the city. One member was elected 'Doge', the ceremonial head of the city.

The Doge's Palace, the ducal home and seat of power for 700 years, was largely constructed from 1309 to 1424 and is a stunning Gothic creation with the canal on one side and St Mark's Square on the other. Next to the palace on St Mark's Square is St Mark's Basilica, the most famous of the city's churches and one of the best-known examples of Byzantine architecture. The cathedral has been the seat of the Patriarch of Venice, archbishop of the Roman Catholic Archdiocese of Venice, since 1807. It is famous for its sheer opulence, and its wonderful gilded Byzantine mosaics. Venice boasts some great works of Renaissance art. The best galleries are the Accademia, the Galleria Giorgio Franchetti in the Gothic Ca' d'Oro and the Peggy Guggenheim Collection.

Venice may be one of the biggest tourist attractions in the world, but however busy it is, few visitors are not overawed by its beauty, elegance and grandeur.

Twilight at the Piazza San Marco

Lake Garda

The Italian lakes are renowned for their sublime beauty, and Lake Garda is the star. It is the largest lake in Italy, 370 sq km (143 sq mi) and 346 m (1,135 ft) deep, with spectacularly blue water and landscapes full of contrast and colour. It lies in an alpine region, halfway between Venice and Milan, in a moraine valley formed by glaciation from the last ice age. It has an exceptionally mild microclimate that supports year-round green vegetation. The Lake acts as a giant solar panel and the heat is prevented from escaping by the surrounding mountains.

From its northern tip, for about two thirds of its length, Lake Garda is a narrow fjord, enclosed by mountains and dominated by the verdant ridge of Monte Baldo, 2,078 m (6,815 ft) high, on its eastern shore. Steep limestone escarpments, covered in woods and pasture, sweep down to the edges of the lake. Winding roads and paths snake their way through isolated villages, past castles and ancient churches perched perilously on the rocky slopes.

Towards the south, it feels much more Mediterranean. The

lake suddenly opens out, widening to 17 km (11 mi) across and the landscape is transformed into gently rolling hills with citrus trees, vines, oleander and bougainvillea. The ancient town of Sirmione juts out on a peninsula at the southern edge, with its quaint cobblestone streets, fairytale 13th-century castle and thermal springs. There are Roman remains here including the villa of the love poet, Catullus.

The Brescia Riviera on the western shore is a well-known holiday hideout for the wealthy and Lake Garda is one of the top resorts in Europe for sailing and windsurfing.

A view of Limone on the shore of Lake Garda

Portofino

If you are looking for the high life come to Portofino, one of Liguria's most exclusive seaside resorts, and also one of its most beautiful. It is situated on an idyllic promontory, its harbour is full of the elegant yachts of the international jet-set and its calm waters reflect the lovely ochre and yellow houses ringed around the water's edge.

The village has long been a favourite with celebrities – Truman Capote and Guy de Maupassant both wrote here; Hollywood stars such as Greta Garbo, Clark Gable, Elizabeth Taylor and Rex Harrison stayed here, the Duke and Duchess of Windsor honeymooned here and Aristotle Onassis arrived on his yacht. Today the rich and famous tend to holiday in private villas up in the hills behind the town but you never know who you might spot hiding behind sunglasses and sipping a Campari and soda at a waterfront bar.

Take the steps up to the Castello Brown, bought by an English diplomat in the 1860s and transformed into a family home. The gardens are lovely and offer great views of the harbour below.

Take a boat trip or a walk across the promontory to the eleventh-century Abbazia di San Fruttuoso, set amongst pine trees and olive groves. Nearby, but out to sea, is a bronze statue of Christ, placed on the sea-bed in 1954 to protect sailors. You can either take a boat to see this, on a calm day, or dive down for a close-up look, if you are not too busy shopping in one of the expensive little boutiques around town.

WHAT IS IT?
One of Liguria's most exclusive seaside resorts.
HIGHLIGHTS:
Rapallo, the church of San Giorgio; Santa Margherita; the five villages of Cinque Terre.

DON'T MISS:
Enjoy the café culture and partake in an afternoon of celebrity spotting.
HOW TO GET THERE:
Travel by bus or ferry from Santa Margherita.

107

Dusk falls on the pretty harbour.

NEXT: The lovely houses add a splash of colour to the harbour.

Florence

POPULATION:
370,000 (2008)
WHEN TO GO:
Spring or autumn
DON'T MISS:
The Duomo – this
cathedral plays a large part
in making Florence's
skyline one of the most
picturesque in the world.
Completed in 1466 after
170 years of work, it holds
up to 30,000 people. Its
domed roof is symbolic of
the meeting of Renaissance
craft and culture and
stands at a height of
114.5m (375 ft).
The Uffizi – one of the
most famous galleries in
the world, the collection of
universally acclaimed
masterpieces on display
here, including works by da
Vinci, Michelangelo and
Rembrandt, is simply
overwhelming.
The Palazzo Pitti.
The Loggia dei Lanzi's
open-air sculptures.
A picnic in the Boboli
Gardens – from here enjoy
the expansive city views as
well as the distinguished
collection of sculptures on
display.
The churches of San
Miniato al Monte, Santa
Maria Novella, Santo Spirito
and Orsanmichele.
YOU SHOULD KNOW:
You can book ahead for the
Uffizi to avoid long queues.

Florence is the cultural centre of Italy, and perhaps of the Western world. Crammed with galleries, wonderful buildings and world-class art treasures, this unspoilt late-medieval city clearly demonstrates its importance in the cultural and political development of Europe. The architectural jewel of Florence has to be the Cathedral of Santa Maria del Fiore, known as the Duomo, a Gothic masterpiece. Its magnificent dome was built by Filippo Brunelleschi, and inside there are beautiful frescoes by some of Italy's greatest artists. The Campanile tower (partly designed by Giotto) and the Baptistery buildings are also well worth a visit. The Baptistery started out as a Roman temple; its bronze doors were among the earliest large bronze castings in the Renaissance period. Both the dome and the tower are open to tourists and provide excellent views over the city rooftops.

At the heart of the city in Piazza della Signoria is the awe-inspiring Fountain of Neptune created by Bartolomeo Ammanati. This famous marble sculpture lies at the end of a Roman aqueduct, still in working order. A stroll around the city streets will reveal many Renaissance architectural masterpieces, including Brunelleschi's Ospedale degli Innocenti (foundling hospice), the Pazzi chapel in the Church of Santa Croce, Michelangelo's work at San Lorenzo, and the Laurentian Library.

Renaissance Florence was dominated by the Medici, the most powerful family in the city from the 15th to the 18th century. They patronized many artists, and the city's two major art galleries, the Uffizi and the Pitti Palace, were created for their art collections. The Uffizi was first opened to visitors in

1591, which makes it one of Europe's first museums. Today it houses the greatest collection of Italian and Florentine art in the world. On the other side of the river is the Pitti Palace, which contains some of the Medici family's private works, as well as a large number of Renaissance masterpieces, including several by Raphael and Titian, and a large collection of modern art. Next to the Palace are the lovely Boboli Gardens, displaying a whole host of interesting sculptures.

The River Arno passes through the centre of Florence, and by wandering along its banks, you can enjoy the unspoiled skyline of domes and towers. Be sure to see the Ponte Vecchio, with its built-in houses and shops. Built in 1345, this is the only bridge in the city to survive World War II.

A view of the Ponte Vecchio

NEXT: Santa Maria del Fiore Cathedral seen from the Hotel Baglioni.

Siena

Surrounded by vineyards and olive groves, Siena sits on the northern edge of the Crete Senese, a landscape of soft, rounded hills bathed in warm,

golden light. One of the most beautiful cities of Tuscany, it is set on three hills linked by a maze of winding alleys and steep steps. The Piazza del Campo, a stunning paved square, stands at the heart of the city, overlooked by the magnificent Duomo.

POPULATION:
54,000 (2008)
WHEN TO GO:
July and August for the Palio.
DON'T MISS:
The Palazzo Pubblico and the Torre del Mangia – the palace was built in the 13th century to house the republican government.
The duomo – this medieval cathedral takes the form of a Latin cross. Both the exterior and interior contain examples of striped black and white marble, the symbolic colours of Siena due to the black and white horses of the city's legendary founders Senius and Aschius.
The Museo dell'Opera del Duomo – houses the best of Siena's paintings and sculptures, including some of the best Italian Gothic and Renaissance art in the country.
The Pinacoteca Nazionale – a wonderful art gallery displaying local art dating from 1200 -1300.
The Piazza del Campo – this shell-shaped piazza lies at the heart of Siena and has served as a focus for life in the city for centuries. It is regarded as one of the most beautiful civic spaces in Europe and is the venue for a medieval horse race that takes place each year in July or August.
The church of San Domenico.
YOU SHOULD KNOW:
There are entrance charges for most historic sites.

The Piazza del Campo   115

A couple wander down Vicolo delle Scotte.

Siena is home to one of the oldest universities in Europe, which lends a bustling, vibrant atmosphere to this historic place.

The city started out as an Etruscan hilltop town, but by 30AD the Romans had established a military outpost here. The Lombards arrived in the 6th century, followed by the Franks. Between the 9th and 11th centuries, the church played an active role in governing the city, but the inhabitants soon claimed their right to govern and administer their town.

The city's wealth and military power grew quickly and friction developed between Siena and Florence, as both cities tried to enlarge their territory. There were many battles between the two cities, but eventually Siena was incorporated into Florentine territory. Despite these turbulent times, in the years 1150–1300 the city flourished and beautiful monuments such as the Duomo, the Palazzo Pubblico and the Torre del Mangia were built. However, a devastating plague hit Siena in 1348 and killed three-fifths of the population, after which the city was slow to recover.

In the centre of the city is the enormous, scallop-shaped Piazza del Campo. One of the greatest squares in the world, it is overlooked by the Palazzo Pubblico and the soaring Torre del Mangia. Collectively, they are a UNESCO World Heritage Site and represent a millennium of Siena's cherished aspiration of independence and (not always successful) democracy.

On the 2 July and the 16 August every year, the Piazza del Campo hosts the Palio, a world-famous bareback horse race round the cobbled streets of the city. Rival processions fill the town, each in their own colourful medieval dress, with screeching bands and flying flags. These races have been run continuously for at least 500 years and are a part of Siena's living history.

The Amalfi Coast

The Amalfi Coast (Costiera Amalfitana) stretches for just 40 km (25 mi) along the south side of the Sorrentine Peninsula, between Positano and Vietri sul Mare, south of the Bay of Naples. It is stunningly beautiful. Backed by the spine of the harsh Lattari

WHAT IS IT?
The Amalfi Coast is a beautiful stretch of coastline 40 km (25 mi) long that runs along the south side of the Sorrentine Peninsula.

WHEN TO GO:
Spring and autumn are best as the area is really crowded in summer.

HIGHLIGHTS:
The gardens of the Villa Cimbrone and Villa Rufolo in Ravello, the old paper mill in Amalfi, the village of Positano and the island of Capri.

DON'T MISS:
Explore the 'Path of the Gods' and walk from Positano to Praiano.

mountains, it consists of vertiginous slopes plunging 210 m (700 ft) into the deep, intensely blue Tyhrrenian Sea. Broken by rocky spurs and ravines into tiny bays and secret coves, it appears to be completely wild and even hostile. But every twist and turn of the switchback coast road reveals a dramatic new vista of ancient fishing villages clinging to the mountainside,

The Italian town of Positano clings to the Amalfi coast.

tumbling down to quayside huddles of colourful boats and café awnings.

Positano is becoming the resort of choice for the rich, powerful and famous. Its multi-coloured houses crowd together, interwoven by a million steps, arcades, and arched passages full of shops, lively bars and excellent restaurants. It is both the prettiest of, and a blueprint for, the other communities dotting the area. Amalfi itself, in the middle of the coast, is still the largest and most influential town here. Only modern tourism has restored to it some of the colossal wealth it used to command. But though Amalfi is as historically fascinating as any of its neighbours (it was once a major naval power with a population of 70,000), its perfect setting now attracts people seeking pleasure and recreation.

The Amalfi Coast's communities look seawards. The switchback coast road was only built in 1850. But whether you see this section of the coast from land or sea, its loveliness is a romantic fantasy come true.

A church in Ravello on the Amalfi Coast

Verona

Strategically located where the River Adage
emerges from the Alps onto the Northern Italian
plain, Verona is near Lake Garda on a loop of the
fast-flowing river. It is a city of bridges (ten of
them) and was once the most important town
owned by Venice on the mainland (terra firma).
Richly endowed with picturesque streets and
squares, art and architecture, it is hardly possible

*This, 'they say' is
Juliet's balcony.*

POPULATION:
265,000 (2008)
WHEN TO GO:
Verona gets crowded in midsummer, so June and September are good for those who like breathing space.
DON'T MISS:
The Natural History Museum, with an exceptional collection of fossils and archaeological remains.
Castelvecchio Museum in a 14th century castle, with superb sculptures, statues and paintings . . . plus a great view of the city's terracotta roofscape from the platform on the keep.
The imposing Gothic tombs of the ruling Scaglier family adjoining the Church of Santa Maria Antica.
Sweeping views from the top of the Torre del Commune (lift, not stairs!).
The Dominican Church of Sant'Anastasia by the river (built in Gothic style 1290-1323) for the wonderfully decorated interior.
Scaligero Bridge, a fine 14th century structure restored after damage in World War II.
YOU SHOULD KNOW:
Verona is the home of ill-starred Romeo and Juliet, and an old stone balcony falsely claiming association with the fictional lovers is a popular attraction.

to imagine a city that has a more appealing character. It is, quite rightly, a UNESCO World Heritage Site.

The city's history is well illustrated by famous monuments and buildings. The amphitheatre built around 30 AD is the third largest in Italy and there are other Roman remains, such as a theatre and the rebuilt Gavi Arch. The 4th century shrine of Verona's patron saint, St Zeno, lies beneath the stunning Basilica of San Zeno Maggiore, a triumph of Romanesque architecture built in the 12th century. Other Romanesque masterpieces include the small Basilica of San Lorenzo, the large Church of Santa Maria Antica and the striking Cathedral, with its fine Gothic interior. Indeed, there are so many fascinating churches in Verona that a month could easily be spent viewing them.

The old town's central feature is the elongated Piazza del Erbe, once the Roman forum and now the scene of a lively market. This must surely be one of the most delightful old squares in all Italy. Nearby Piazza dei Signori is surrounded by palaces, including one now serving as the Town Hall. The Loggia del Consiglio is one of the finest early Renaissance buildings in the country, crowned by statues of famous Veronans. The city walls are a 15th century architectural statement, that were built to serve both a defensive and aesthetic function – marvel at the Porta del Palio.

Rome

In central Italy where the River Aniene joins the Tiber lies Rome, a powerful political and economic centre for 2,500 years. Not only does the city ooze history, both ancient and more modern, it is also the capital of a thoroughly sophisticated and forward-thinking nation. Most visitors are awestruck by the sheer pace of life here, mainly fuelled by espresso coffee, but there are also moments of tranquil reflection. Whether shopping

The Temple of Aesculapius in the Villa Borghese Gardens

POPULATION:
2,600,000 (2005)
WHEN TO GO:
Any time of year.
DON'T MISS:
The Palatine Hill – an
open-air museum with
wonderful views of
the Forum.
The Forum – this huge
site (a good map is
advisable!) is where
public meetings would
have been held and
famous orators would
have spoken. This is
where Mark Anthony
delivered his speech
following the
assassination of Caesar.
The Castel Sant'Angelo
– originally
commissioned by
Roman Emperor Hadrian
as a mausoleum for
himself and his family
and located on the
banks of the Tiber, this
is one of Rome's finest
sights.
The Spanish Steps –
these 138 steps join the
Piazza di Spanga and
the Trinita dei Monti
church and were
designed in 1723. The
house at the base of
the steps is where the
poet John Keats lived
YOU SHOULD KNOW:
Most tourist attractions
have entrance fees.

*A couple admires the
Colosseum at night.*

125

on the Via Veneto, visiting ancient ruins or admiring the work of Leonardo Da Vinci, visitors very rarely go away disappointed.

Rome is one of the few major European cities that escaped World War II relatively intact, so central Rome remains essentially Renaissance and Baroque in character. With more than 900 churches and basilicas, it has been for centuries the centre of the Christian world. Among the most important of the churches are San Giovanni in Laterano, Santa Maria Maggiore and San Lorenzo Fuori le Mura.

In the middle of Rome is Vatican City, a separate sovereign state and the enclave of the Holy See. Here is Saint Peter's Basilica and its huge forecourt designed under the direction of Pope Alexander VII so that the greatest number of people could see the Pope give his blessing from the façade of the church. In Vatican City there are also the prestigious Vatican Library, the Raphael Rooms and other important works by Leonardo Da Vinci, Raphael, Giotto and Botticelli. The Vatican Museums, founded by Pope Julius II in the sixteenth century, display works from the fabulous and extensive collection of the Roman Catholic Church, including the world-famous Sistine Chapel.

Rome boasts a wealth of important art treasures to tempt the visitor. The best an be found in the Galleria Borghese, the Palazzo Doria Pamphili, the Capitoline museums, the Museo Nazionale delle Terme, the Galleria Colonna, and the Palazzo Barberini with its National Gallery of Antique Art.

The ancient Roman ruins are, of course, among the best in the world. The highlights include the sumptuous imperial palaces on the Palatine Hill, the temples in the forum, Augustus' Ara Pacis (altar of peace), the huge Baths of Diocletian, the exquisite Pantheon, the eerie catacombs and the chill of the Colosseum where, like the Circus Maximus, a discontented population was kept in check by often bloodthirsty public spectacles.

The Dalmatian Coast

A view of Rab

The rugged Dalmatian coastline is an exquisite stretch of more than 1,780 km (1,100 mi) of intricate coves, channels and inlets, fringed by a complex network of more than a thousand islands. It runs along the eastern shores of the Adriatic Sea, from the island of Rab in the northwest to the Gulf of Kotor in the southeast, with a hinterland that is only 50 km (30 mi) at its widest point.

There are hundreds of glorious unspoilt beaches, seven national parks and some of the most beautiful

127

WHAT IS IT?
Magnificent and varied
coastline and popular
holiday destination.
HOW TO GET THERE:
Fly to Zagreb. Domestic
flight to Split or Dubrovnik,
or high-speed train to Split.
Jadrolinija coastal ferry plies
the waters between
Dubrovnik
and Rijeka.
WHEN TO GO:
April to October.
NEAREST TOWNS:
Rijeka, Zadar, Split,
Dubrovnik.

medieval towns and villages in Europe. From space, the Adriatic is the bluest patch of sea on the planet.

Each island has a unique charm of its own. The stark white karst (limestone) cliffs of the barren 'Robinson Crusoe' Kornati islands stand out in spectacular contrast to the cobalt blue seas. Krapanj, famous for its sponges, is a peaceful haven for a secluded holiday. Hvar is the place for celebrity spotting, and the beach of Brac is renowned among surfers. The green, hilly island of Korkula was Marco Polo's birthplace, and the beautiful forests of Mjlet are a National Park.

The extraordinary geological complexity of the Dalmatian coastline is the result of 'concordance'. Where two bands of rock run parallel to the coast, the outer band may be harder than the inner. The surface of the hard outer rock cracks at weak spots, allowing water to seep in, which dissolves the softer rock from the inside. Inlets, and coves with characteristic narrow entrances, are formed and islands break away from the mainland. named 'Destination of the Year' by *National Geographic* magazine, the Dalmatian Coast has a growing reputation as 'the New Riviera'. With its balmy Mediterranean climate, magical beauty and fascinating history, one can see why.

DON'T MISS:
Dubrovnik, described by Byron as 'the pearl of the Adriatic'. The island of Mljet's two interconnected salt-water lakes, Malo Jezero and Veliko Jezero, and 12th century Benedictine Monastery.

The red-tiled roofs of Dubrovnik

Paxi and Andipaxi

POPULATION:
2,500 (2001)
WHEN TO GO:
May, June, September and October
HOW TO GET THERE:
Ferry from the mainland (Igoumenitsa); hydrofoil from Corfu.
HIGHLIGHTS:
Walking is a good way to get to know the islands; good maps and guides are available.
Boat trips – the boat from Paxi to Andipaxi may visit some of the most dramatic caves in the region.
YOU SHOULD KNOW:
The statue on Gaios waterfront commemorates a Paxiot sailor who tried to set fire to the Turkish fleet.

Paxi is a tiny island, and has no spectacular sandy beaches or historical sites; its limited accommodation is block-booked in season, and its popularity with yacht flotillas has pushed prices up. However, visitors fall in

Boats moored near Lakka.

love with it. Largely unspoilt – its tourism is run by small, discriminating companies – it is beautiful, friendly and charming.

The east coast is characterized by low hills and shingly coves, the west by precipitous cliffs above inaccessible caves and beaches. There are three coastal

A view of Lakka through the olive trees

settlements. Gaios, the capital and main port, is a pleasant, attractive town of old, red-roofed, pastel-washed buildings around a seafront square, with views of two islets. Longos to the northwest is a pretty fishing village and a quieter resort. Picturesque Lakka sits on a beautiful horseshoe bay at the north of the island. It has a couple of beaches and some good walks. Inland Paxi, with its ancient olive groves and scattering of farms and villages, is perfect walking country. The one main road runs down the spine of the island.

Andipaxi, with its gorgeous sandy coves and dazzlingly blue water, can be reached by excursion boat from any of the resorts. The beaches do get busy, but it is possible to walk across the islet (it is covered in vines, and produces good wine) to quieter bays.

Santorini

In the southern Aegean Sea, about 200 km south of mainland Greece, lies Santorini, a spectacular volcanic island in the Cyclades group known for its dramatic views, brilliant sunsets and fine beaches. The beauty of the island and its dynamic nightlife have made this a popular tourist destination.

From above it is obvious that the island, shaped like a ring with a huge bay of sea in the centre, is what remains of a giant volcano which erupted in around 1650 BC, one of the biggest volcanic explosions the earth has ever seen. The walls of the caldera surrounding the bay in the centre rise a sheer 300 m out of the sea. The traces of previous eruptions can be seen in the coloured bands of rock on the island's cliffs: each one is a layer of compressed ash ejected in one eruption. The small island in the middle of the bay is another volcanic cone forming.

The very picturesque town of of Oia

POPULATION:
13,670 (2001)
WHEN TO GO:
April to October
HOW TO GET THERE:
By ferry from the Greek
mainland or other Greek
islands, or by plane from
Athens, Thessaloniki and a
few other European cities.
HIGHLIGHTS:
The excavations at Akrotiri
– this Minoan town was
buried by lava during the
volcanic eruption, and the
excavations have revealed
multi-level buildings and
beautiful frescoes.
The Archaeological Museum
at Thira – the story of
Akrotiri and other ancient
settlements on the island is
told through Neolithic and
Bronze Age artefacts.
The beaches – the best
beach is probably that at
Perissa, but the black sand
beach in the charming town
of Kamari also makes a nice
day out.
Mesa Gonia – a small village
with lovely traditional
architecture, some ruins
from the 1956 earthquake,
restored villas and a winery.
Pyrgos – an inland village
with some grand houses, a
ruined Venetian castle and
some Byzantine churches.
YOU SHOULD KNOW:
The island is also
sometimes referred to as
Thira.

Evidence suggests that the massive eruption caused
a tsunami which led indirectly to the decline of the
Minoan civilization centred on nearby Crete. The
Minoan settlement on Santorini itself was engulfed in
lava and the stunning remains, at Akrotiri, make a
fascinating day out. There are three-storey houses with
magnificent frescos,
ceramics and staircases,
and the hot and cold running
water system suggests this
was a prosperous and
refined town.

Thira is the island's
capital, perched high up on
the cliffs 300 m (984 ft)
above its port below. Its
architecture is an attractive
mix of Venetian and
traditional Cycladic and the
white cobblestone streets are
lined with shops and cafés.
Thira can get busy in
summer as cruise ships dock
here while the passengers
explore the town. There are
three main means of getting
from the port up to the town
– by cablecar, by donkey, or
by walking up the 300-odd
zigzagging steps.

The town of Ia
(sometimes spelled Oia),
with its pretty whitewashed
buildings and blue domes, is
one of the most charming

places on the island, albeit rather busy with tourists. The town offers views of the open sea to the east, as well as the bay to the west, and many people congregate here in the late afternoon to watch the sunset over the bay, a really memorable experience.

The perfect spot for a glass of wine

Istanbul

Istanbul is an utterly bewitching city – a
mesmerising, schizoid medley of sumptuous
palaces, domes and minarets, cobble-stoned streets,
decrepit old wooden houses, squalid concrete tower
blocks, graceful art nouveau apartments,

international fashion shops, bazaars and beggars, street vendors and stray dogs and, above all, the boats of the Bosphorus and the promise of the Orient.

A city has been here since the year dot, bridging the gap between Europe and Asia. Over the centuries, it has been the capital of the Roman,

The Ayasofya dominates the city.

POPULATION:
10,291,000 (2007)

WHEN TO GO:
Spring or autumn. The summer months are very hot and it often snows in the winter.

DON'T MISS:
Taking a cruise up the Bosphorus and admire the *yali* lining the shore – old wooden mansions, once the summerhouses of wealthy Istanbullus.

The experience of a genuine Turkish bath in the Çemberlitas or the Cagaloglu hamams.

A tour of the Dolmabahçe Sarayi – a sumptuous palace with the largest chandelier in Europe.

The atmosphere of the Egyptian Spice Market and surrounding streets.

The buzzing port area of Karaköy, with the Balik Pazari fish and vegetable market, cheap local restaurants and street food.

The Ortakoy Mosque and area.

YOU SHOULD KNOW:
Some of Istanbul is extremely poor. Like all major cities, it attracts immigrants in search of work, many of whom are living in *gecekondus* – illegally built squatters' dwellings on the outskirts of the city. Do not let western prejudices and annoyance at street hustlers get in the way of your appreciation of the city.

Byzantine and Ottoman Empires and undergone three name changes – Byzantium, Constantinople, Istanbul. After the Republic of Turkey was founded in 1923, it was replaced by Ankara as the capital, but, with its awe-inspiring heritage, Istanbul remains Turkey's cultural and economic centre.

Istanbul straddles the Bosphorus Strait, looking towards Europe but with its soul firmly rooted in Asia. On the European side, the city is divided once more, north and south of the Golden Horn inlet. In the south are the superb World Heritage sites of the Blue Mosque, the magnificent 15th century Topkapi Palace, and Ayasofya – the 'mother of churches', a masterpiece of Byzantine architecture. Here too is the Grand Bazaar, Kapali Çarsi, a vast labyrinth of narrow covered passageways selling everything from cheap tat to carpets worth thousands. Only a few minutes walk is Suleymaniye Caami, a spectacular Ottoman Mosque, and, further west, the old city walls and the beautiful Kariye Camii.

North of the Galata Bridge, there is a magnificent 14th century Genoese landmark, Galata Kulesi, with a fantastic view. From here, the city takes on a distinctly European guise. The main boulevard, Istiklal Caddesi – lined with superb *fin-de-siècle* architecture – leads up to Taksim and the impressive Monument of the Republic.

Everywhere you turn in this compelling city, you stumble over the melancholic remains of a magnificent imperial past – neglected, ignored bits of history. Istanbul enchants the traveller with haunting memories – the breathtaking interior of the Blue Mosque, the smells and clatter of the fish market, the tiny boats vying with huge tankers in the Bosphorus – apparently fleeting impressions that remain forever.

Prague

Prague has been the political, cultural, and economic centre of the Czech state for over 1000 years. Lying on a bend in the River Vltava, half-way between Berlin and Vienna, it is set on seven hills topped by lovely castles and churches. Prague is widely considered to be one of the most beautiful cities in Europe. In 1993, after the split of Czechoslovakia, Prague became the capital city of the new Czech Republic. Since the end of Communism, Prague has become one of the most visited cities in Europe, famous for its café culture and vibrant nightlife in the most beautiful surroundings.

The city's heyday was during the fourteenth century and the reign of Charles IV. Charles founded the first university in central, northern and eastern Europe, today known as the Charles University. He also founded New Town, adjacent to the Old Town, rebuilt Prague Castle and Vysehrad, and erected Charles Bridge. Under his reign, many new churches were built, including St Vitus' Cathedral, and Charles was crowned Emperor of the Holy Roman Empire. He wanted Prague to be one of the most beautiful cities in the world, dominating the whole empire, with Prague Castle dominating the city and the Gothic Cathedral dominating the castle. To this end, he created many beautiful buildings which are still with us today.

The castle was founded in the 9th century, and has since remained the seat of power. It is one of the largest castles in the world, and houses the crown jewels of the Bohemian Kingdom. Just outside is the eighteenth-century Sternberg Palace (Sternbersk ẙ palác), home to the National Gallery with its superb collection of Old Masters. The complex also contains the wonderful Royal Gardens and the stately Gothic St Vitus' Cathedral, begun in 1344. The walls of the

POPULATION:
1,198,000 (2007)
WHEN TO GO:
March to April, or September to November.
DON'T MISS:
The Old Town Hall – famous for its astronomical clock; on the hour every hour enjoy the procession of the twelve apostles who emerge from a small trap door.
The synagogues of Josefov – this site in the Jewish Quarter consists of six synagogues and a cemetary commemorating the killing of the Jews in 1270. Visiting is a highly emotional experience.
Wallenstein Garden – many concerts are held here in the summer months.
Vysehrad Castle, perched on a cliff high above the Vltava River.
Nové Město the 'New City'.
Crossing the Charles Bridge.
YOU SHOULD KNOW:
Entrance fees are payable at most tourist attractions.

Crossing the Charles Bridge at sunset.

chapel that houses the tomb of St Wenceslas are lined with precious stones and beautiful paintings.

Prague's old town (Staré Město) is an atmospheric area of cobbled streets, alleyways, superb churches and palaces. The Little Quarter (Malá Strana) lies

below the castle walls. This district features many
notable historic buildings, among them St Nicholas
Cathedral. The Charles Bridge is another must-see.
Built in 1357 with a tower at either end, it offers
spectacular views of the city to those who cross it.

Bled

Known in Slovenia as the 'alpine pearl', Bled is a particularly attractive small town in a fairy-tale location. Set against the backdrop of the forested slopes of the Julian Alps in north-west Slovenia, and the peaks of the Karavanke Mountains, it sits beside a beautiful emerald-green lake with an island in the middle and looming over all, perched high up on the rocky cliff on the northern side of town is the awe-inspiring red-and-white Castle of Bled, the origins of which date back to the eleventh century. It was rebuilt in the seventeenth century, renovated and remodelled in the 1950s and now houses a museum.

Once home to the Yugoslav royal family, famous as a health spa at the beginning of the twentieth century and later the summer residence of President Tito, Bled has naturally always been something of a magnet for visitors – from the pilgrims of many centuries ago to the honeymooners of today.

On the island in Lake Bled there is a picturesque little white seventeenth-century church complete with a wishing bell. Legend has it that a husband who can carry his new bride up the 99 stone steps from the dock to the church will enjoy a happy marriage and ringing the bell will make the couple's dreams come true.

WHEN TO GO:
Arrive in July for Rikli's festival, when thousands of lighted candles float on the lake.
HOW TO GET THERE:
By road or rail from Ljubljana.
HIGHLIGHTS:
Lake Bohinj – 30 km (19 mi) south-west of Bled, hiking in Triglav National Park, wandering around the Old Town in Ljubljana.
DON'T MISS:
Take a horse-drawn carriage ride around the lake.

This church on the island in Lake Bled is the place to go for newlyweds!

St Petersburg

POPULATION:
4,700,000 (2006)
WHEN TO GO:
May to July.
DON'T MISS:
Nevsky Prospekt.
The Russian Museum –
home to the world's largest
collection of Russian fine
art.
Alexander Nevsky
Monastery.
The Steiglitz Museum.
Yusupov's Palace – one of
St Petersburg's most
beautiful buildings both
inside and out. Its cellar
was the place where
Rasputin, one of Russia's
most scandalous figures,
was murdered. The palace
houses a Rasputin
exhibition.
YOU SHOULD KNOW:
The city centre is a UNESCO
World Heritage Site.

Described by Dostoevsky as' the most artificial city in the world', St Petersburg was founded by Tsar Peter the Great in 1703 as the capital of the Russian Empire, which it remained for more than two hundred years until the government moved to Moscow after the revolution of 1917. This is a beautiful city with a rich history, and offers many treats for lovers of art and architecture.

Tsar Peter built the city after reconquering the Ingrian land from Sweden at the beginning of the Great Northern War. He named it after his patron saint, the apostle Saint Peter, and envisaged it as a great city dedicated to art and culture. He chose a site on what was then a large swamp, the delta of the Neva River, on the edge of the Baltic Sea's Gulf of Finland. Due to the adverse weather and geographical conditions, there was a high mortality rate among workers on his new city, so Peter levied a yearly conscription of 40,000 peasants from all parts of the country. Half of them died or escaped on the long trek there.

The Neva River, with its many canals and their granite embankments and bridges, sets St Petersburg apart from other Russian cities. Dominated by the Baroque Winter Palace, stretching 200 m (660 ft) along the river front, it is imbued with Russian imperial history. Commissioned by Tsarina Elizabeth, the lavish interior of the palace reflects the opulent lives of the tsars. Catherine the Great added the Hermitage in 1764 to house her private art collection, now one of the largest in the world.

The main street in the city is Nevsky Prospekt, along which there are many rewarding sights. These include the Rastrelliesque Stroganov Palace, a monument to Catherine the Great, the Art Nouveau Bookhouse, the Anichkov Bridge with its remarkable horse statues, several eighteenth-century churches, an enormous

eighteenth-century shopping centre, a nineteenth-century department store and the fascinating Russian National Library.

There are dozens of Baroque and Neoclassical palaces in the city, and an amazing array of churches. The astonishing St Isaac's Cathedral has an enormous dome covered with gold, and the Cathedral of Peter and Paul in Palace Square contains the tombs of Peter the Great and his successors. The huge neoclassical Kazan Cathedral on Nevsky Prospekt is modelled on St Peter's in Rome and well worth a visit. The Alexander Nevsky Monastery comprises two cathedrals and five churches in various styles. It is also known for its cemetery, with the graves of many well-known figures, such as Dostoyevsky, Krylov, Ilyich, Tchaykovsky and Mussorgsky.

Empress Maria Alexandrovna's Boudoir in the Winter Palace

NEXT: The facade and gardens of Catherine Palace

ROMANTIC GETAWAYS IN
ASIA

Samarkand

POPULATION:
590,000 (2008)
WHEN TO GO:
April to June, or September
to October.
DON'T MISS:
The Gur-e Amir.
Shah-i-Zinda.
The madrasahs of Ulugh Beg,
Sherdar and Tilla Kari.
The Bibi Khanum Mosque.
YOU SHOULD KNOW:
This is one of the oldest and
most important cities of
Asia.

Capturing the town on his way to India, Alexander the Great described Samarkand as 'more beautiful than he had imagined'. In the fourteenth century, Timur Gurkani made the city the capital of his empire which stretched from India to Turkey. He turned the city into a magnificent centre of mosques and mausoleums, which was spoken of as 'the precious pearl of the world'. Today Samarkand is the third largest city in Uzbekistan, and is home to a dazzling array of architecture and culture representing its long and sometimes violent history.

Samarkand lies in a strategic position in the Zarafshan Valley on the ancient Silk Road, which helps to explain its turbulent past and mixture of cultures. The city has been won and lost by a great number of different powers over the centuries, including the Persians, Alexander the Great, the Arabs, Genghis Khan, Timur Gurkani (Tamerlane the Great), the Turks and the Russians. This led to a unique culture with Persian, Indian and Mongolian influences, a little of the West and the East.

Built after the death of Timur's grandson Muhammad-Sultan in 1403, the Gur-e Amir became the family mausoleum of the Timurid Dynasty. The fantastic blue ribbed dome dominates the skyline of central Samarkand. Inside, the broken, gigantic slab of jade commemorating the mighty Timur is said to be the largest jade stone in the world. One of the most beautiful of Samarkand's sights, Shah-i-Zinda (the tomb of the living king) houses the shrine of Prophet Muhammad's cousin, Qusam ibn Abbas, who brought Islam to the region. This is one of the oldest structures in Samarkand and a popular pilgrimage site.

Other notable sights include the Registan, a huge square in the centre of the city, surrounded on three sides by three universities: the medieval Ulugh Beg, the Sherdar and the Tilla Kari Madrasahs. Decorated inside and out with glazed bricks, intricate blue and turquoise mosaics and carved marble, these are perhaps the finest Islamic monuments in the world.

The Bibi Khanum Mosque is another architectural gem. It is one of the largest and most grandiose buildings in Samarkand, and its dome is the largest in the Muslim world. Most of the building collapsed in an earthquake in 1897 but it has now been restored by the Russian Government.

Sha-i-Zinda is one of Samarkand's most beautiful sites.

A boy rides a camel across the shallow Yamuna River by the Taj Mahal

The Taj Mahal

Located outside the city of Agra in the north Indian state of Uttar Pradesh, the Taj Mahal is one of the most beautiful architectural masterpieces in the world. Shah Jahan, a Mughal ruler, ordered the construction of the Taj Mahal in honour of his wife, Arjumand Banu, to commemorate their 18 years of marriage and her death

in childbirth with their fourteenth child. As a testament
to his love for his wife he commissioned the most
beautiful mausoleum on Earth.

The architect of the Taj Mahal is not known for
certain, but Ustad Ahmad Lahori, an Indian architect of
Persian descent, has been widely credited. Construction
began in 1630 when the best masons, craftsmen,
sculptors and calligraphers were summoned from Persia,
the Ottoman Empire and throughout Europe.

WHAT IS IT?
One of the most beautiful
architectural masterpieces in
the world.
WHERE IS IT:
Outside the city of Agra,
200 km (124 mi) south
of Delhi.

The site, on the south-west bank of the River Yamuna outside Agra, has five main structures: the Darwaza, or main gateway; the Bageecha, or garden; the Masjid or mosque; the Naqqar Khana, or rest house and the Rauza, the mausoleum, where the tomb is located.

The unique Mughal style combines elements of Persian, Central Asian and Islamic architecture. Highlights include the black-and-white marble checked floor, the four 40-m (656-ft) minarets at the corners of the mausoleum's plinth and its majestic middle dome.

The lettering of the Qur'anic verses around the archways appears to be uniform in height no matter how far it is from the ground, an optical effect caused by increasing the size and spacing of the letters higher up. Other optical effects can be spotted throughout the Taj. The impressive *pietra dura* artwork includes geometric elements as well as plants and flowers, mostly common in Islamic architecture. The level of sophistication and intricacy of the monument becomes apparent when you take the time to examine the small details – for instance, in some places, one 3-cm (1.2-in) decorative element contains more than 50 inlaid gemstones.

The Taj Mahal truly is a great work of art.

A couple visit the Taj Mahal.

Women socializing at Lake Pichola.

Udaipur

Rajasthan is renowned for its beautiful cities, but Udaipur, the 'City of Lakes', must be the most romantic of them all – a gleaming fantasy of 17th and 18th century palaces, temples, gardens, havelis (courtyard houses), bazaars and museums, all in the most wonderful waterside setting.

According to legend, the Rajput Maharana of Mewar, Udai Singh, was out hunting one day when he met a holy man meditating on a hill who told him it was a favourable spot. So in 1559 he decided to build a palace here and in 1568 made Udaipur the capital of his kingdom.

POPULATION:
559,000 (2001)
WHEN TO GO:
September to March.
DON'T MISS:
City Museum.
Jagdish Mandir – largest
temple in Udaipur, with
music and chanting
throughout the day.
Bharatiya Lok Kala Mandal –
excellent folk art museum.
Bagore-ki Haveli – a lovely
18th century residence on
the waterfront where you
can see displays of
Rajasthani dancing and
music.
Fateh Prakash – palace with
crystal collection and jewel-
studded carpet.
Eklingji – 8th century temple
complex with 108
sandstone and marble
temples 22 km (14 mi) from
Udaipur.
YOU SHOULD KNOW:
Udaipur was the birthplace
of Bagheera, the black
panther, in Kipling's *The
Jungle Book*. Udaipur was
ranked 7th top city in the
world 2007 by *Travel &
Leisure* magazine.

A boat ride on Lake Pichola in the setting sun is
enough to quicken the senses of even the most jaded
tourist. There are two islands, on which stand
gleaming white magical palaces – the Jag Niwas and
the Jag Mandir. The lake is enclosed by hills, and the
City Palace runs along the eastern bank. This
magnificent building is one of the largest marble
palaces in the world – a maze of courtyards, terraces,
hanging gardens, cupolas and luxurious apartments.

To the north, the manmade Fateh Sagar lake has a
beautiful island – the Nehru Garden, a huge fountain,
and the Udaipur Solar Observatory. Perched on the

hillside overlooking the city, is the Monsoon Palace, the royal summer residence. And from the Sajjan Niwas garden, a short climb takes you up to the ridge of the old city wall from where you can gaze down over the plains.

In the old city, the curlicued stucco work and colourful painting round the doorways of the whitewashed havelis is straight out of a picture book. Cows and elephants wander around the narrow cobblestoned lanes of the bazaars where artisans ply their trade. Udaipur really is a fairytale city, 'like no other place on earth'.

The City Palace was built on the shore of Lake Pichola.

Srinagar

POPULATION:
895,000 (2001)
WHEN TO GO:
June to September.
DON'T MISS:
A *shikara* ride on Dal Lake.
Mughal Gardens.
Khanqah of Shah Hamadan,
the first mosque built
in Srinagar.

Surrounded by snow-capped peaks and beautiful lakes, the lovely city of Srinagar in the valley of Kashmir has one of the most pleasant climates in India. This is why it has been a popular summer retreat for centuries, attracting the wealthy from the plains of India travelling to avoid the oppressive heat. This was a popular getaway for the Mughal emperors who left their mark in the form of beautiful mosques

and stunning gardens.

Srinagar lies on the banks of the Jhelum River, a tributary of the Indus. A lively, vibrant place with a number of stunning parks, it is well known for the nine ancient bridges that connect the two parts of the city on opposite banks of the river. The city is famous for its lovely lakes, particularly Dal Lake, and the pretty houseboats floating on them. Be sure to take a boat tour of the lake inlets to get a glimpse of the life and wildlife along its banks.

Paddling a shikara *or water taxi on Dal Lake at dawn.*

A flower vendor paddles his merchandise from houseboat to houseboat on Dal Lake.

The Mughal Gardens are among the highlights of a visit to Srinagar. They include Chasma Shahi, the royal fountains; Pari Mahal, the palace of the fairies; Nishat Bagh, the garden of spring; Sahlimar Bagh on the banks of Dal Lake, built by Emperor Jahangir; and the Nashim Bagh.

The city of Srinagar reflects the cultural heritage and religious diversity of the surrounding state of Jammu and Kashmir. This can be seen in the holy sites in and around the city. On a hill to the south-east of the city is the Hindu Shankaracharya Temple, dedicated to Shiva. It was built in 371 BC by Gopadatya, and offers great views of the city. The Hazrathbal shrine is one of the most revered pilgrimage sites in Islam as it houses the sacred hair of Muhammad (Moi-e-Muqqadas). Sadiq Khan laid out a garden here in 1623 on the left bank of Dal Lake and constructed a Pleasure House. Situated in the old city and large enough to accommodate 30,000 worshippers, the Jama Masjid Mosque was built in 1398 by Mughal Sultan Sikandar and is also worth a look.

Suzhou

Perhaps now best known for its traditional waterside architecture and beautiful gardens, Suzhou was the capital of the Wu kingdom for more than eight centuries and a centre of the silk industry. It is often referred to as the Venice of the East.

At almost every turn, you come across a pagoda or a beautiful garden. The gardens were listed as a UNESCO World Heritage Site in 1997. Among the best are the Humble Administrator's Garden (Zhou Zheng Yuan), the Garden of the Master of the Nets (Wang Shi Yuan), the Mountain Villa with Embracing Beauty (Huanxiu Shanzhuang) which is one of the most important water and rock gardens and the Surging Wave Pavilion (Canglangting). There are smaller gardens dotted throughout the city and these are usually more peaceful places to relax. Among the best of these is the Wufeng Xianguan and Yi Yuan.

POPULATION:
6,298,000 (2008)
WHEN TO GO:
Spring or autumn
DON'T MISS:
The Classical Gardens.
Pin Jiang Road – take a stroll along this beautiful ancient road paved with hand-cut stones over 1,000 years old.
Huangcangyu Nature Reserve – the most attractive sight in Suzhou with forests, caves, springs, pools and temples.
Wuliu Scenic Area.
Baita East Road – this street remains undeveloped so maintains many Ming era store fronts.

Traditional riverside houses in Suzhou

The traditional buildings of the city include the Beisi, North and Yunyan pagodas, the Cold Mountain Temple, the Pan Gate and the Baodai Bridge.

Suzhou is also renowned for its arts and crafts. The Kunqu form of Chinese opera originates here, and Suzhou Pingtan is a local storytelling tradition that involves singing. Silk and embroidery are important crafts, as is jade carving.

For a taste of old China, with all its culture and traditions set in a beautiful landscape, this is the place to be.

A water village on the outskirts of Suzhou.

The Three Gorges

Situated in Hubei province, roughly at the halfway point of the Yangtze River, is the famously scenic area of the Three Gorges. The Qutang Gorge is 8 km (5 mi) long, never more than 100 m (330 ft) wide, with almost vertical cliff walls rising up into the clouds. Wu Gorge is 45 km (28 mi) long, and lined with such fantastic cliffs that legend tells of the goddess Yao Ji and her sisters having to turn some wicked river dragons into mountains. Finally, there is Xiling Gorge, at 66 km (41 mi) the longest of the three, and historically considered the most dangerous to navigate.

This area is not only spectacular to look at, but is also bursting with cultural history and many important archaeological sites. For 90 years Chinese governments have been considering putting a dam in these gorges, and the resulting construction, completed in 2006, is the largest hydroelectric river dam in the world.

The new dam has caused enormous controversy. Proponents point to the clean electricity it will provide, desperately needed by the booming economy, and say that it will help to control the ever more frequent flooding that occurs on the Yangtze River. Opponents point to the one million plus displaced people, the loss of hundreds of archaeological sites, 13 cities, 140 towns and 1,352 villages. They say that the ecosystem will be irreparably damaged, that there is a possibility that the reservoir may silt up, causing, rather than preventing, floods, and that the dam has been sited on a seismic fault. It will take some years before we know whether this was a brilliant idea, or a disastrous one.

WHAT IS IT?
Three beautiful gorges on the Yangtze River. However, the largest hydroelectric project in the world, set in the midst of the Yangtze River has been constructed here.
HOW TO GET THERE:
Fly to Chongqing, take a cruise.
WHEN TO GO:
October to March
NEAREST TOWN:
Chongqing, at the southern end of the Three Gorges.

NEXT: *The spectacular Three Gorges*

Hangzhou

POPULATION:
3,932,000 (2003)
WHEN TO GO:
Any time of year.
DON'T MISS:
A trip out to the West Lake's islands.
The silk market on Tiyuchang Road.
Spending an afternoon in a traditional tea house.
The ferry ride down the Grand Canal. This is the longest man-made waterway in China, at 1,764 km (1,200 mi), and taking a ferry ride down it is a great way to take in the traditional river towns and experience local culture.
The Buddhist carvings in the Feilai Feng Caves – the 300 stone carvings here in Hangzhou's most famous site date from 907 to 1368.
YOU SHOULD KNOW:
Marco Polo claims to have come here and described the city as 'beyond dispute the finest and noblest in the world'.

One of the most important cultural centres of China, Hangzhou is also particularly known for its spectacular scenery, which has been described in poetry and painting for centuries. It lies within the Yangtze Delta, on the banks of the Quitang River and at the end of the Grand Canal, so water features large.

West Lake (Xi Hu) is the area's greatest attraction and it is famed for its Ten Prospects and Ten New Prospects, which are said to be the most beautiful, but, to be frank, it is spectacular from just about every direction. Many of the islands, all but one of which are artificial, have temples, palaces, pavilions and pagodas. The most visited attractions here include the Ling Yin Temple, Solitary Hill, the Six

Harmonies Pagoda and the Mausoleum of General Yue Fei. Baochu Pagoda is at the top of the hill to the north of the lake, but is worth the walk. Huanglong Cave is another popular destination in this area.

Several of the museums in the district are devoted to the region's products including the National Silk Museum and the Tea Museum.

The villages of Longjin, Manjuelong and Meijiawu are good places to go to see tea being picked.

Guo's Villa (Guo Zhuang) is a beautiful traditional private garden, one of the best in the region, using the traditions of Taoism to create a harmonious mix of water, open and enclosed spaces, light and shade which eventually opens out to overlook the lake.

Hangzhou is one of the most beautiful places in the world.

The beautiful West Lake

Stunning temples and shrines give Nikko it's UNESCO World Heritage Site status.

Nikko

Just two hours' journey west of Tokyo lies the pilgrimage town of Nikko. It is set within stunning mountain scenery, but its importance lies in its Buddhist and Shinto temples and shrines, which were declared a UNESCO World Heritage Site in 1999.

Three of the most important of these are the Futarasan Jinja, Rinnoji and Nikko Toshogu. The first two belong to the second part of the 8th century, when the Buddhist monk, Shodo, built several shrines, temples and other buildings here, but perhaps the most famous of the three is the Toshogu, a shrine built in honour of the powerful Shogun, Tokugawa Ieyasu after his death in 1616. The first shrine in his honour was relatively simple, but his grandson, Tokugawa Iemitsu, later erected the much more elaborate shrine we see today, covered in carvings and paintings, as well as a highly ornate one for himself. Their grandeur emphasizes the power the Tokugawa Dynasty once held.

The area is also full of other monument, including Torii, beautiful bridges, ornamental bell towers, gateways, pagodas, statues, hallways and other temples and shrines. The Nikko Toshogu Shrine Museum of Art is also here. The Tosho-gu complex lies within a beautiful landscape, with views of the surrounding countryside, which is among the most spectacular in Japan.

POPULATION:
92,000 (2008)
WHEN TO GO:
April to October.
DON'T MISS:
The three wise monkeys carving on the Nikko Toshogo.
Nikko National Park, west of the city, an area of outstanding beauty.
The region's hot springs.
The annual recreation of Ieyasu's funeral rites in May.
YOU SHOULD KNOW:
It can get very cold here in winter.

Kyoto

POPULATION:
1,474,000 (2008)
WHEN TO GO:
Spring, summer or autumn.
DON'T MISS:
The Imperial Palace.
The traditional townhouses
and cobbled lanes of
Sannenzaka
and Ninenzaka.
Toji and Sanjusangendo
Buddhist temples.
Shgakuin imperial villa.
YOU SHOULD KNOW:
The Kyoto Protocol was
signed here in 2002, with
objectives set out to reduce
greenhouse gases and
prevent climate change.

If you conjure up a mental image of traditional
Japanese architecture and gardens, it's likely that it's a
fairly close match to the historic areas of Kyoto. It
was the capital of Japan from 794 until the 1860s,
when Emperor Meiji relocated to Edo. It is one of the
few cities in Japan to retain large numbers of older
buildings, and 17 properties here, consisting of 198
monuments, make up the UNESCO World Heritage
Site of the Historic Monuments of Kyoto, which was
declared in 1994. Among the best known of these are
Kinkaku-ji (the Golden Pavilion) and Gingaku-ji (the
Silver Pavilion). The latter is a beautiful, two-storey
wooden pavilion set among traditional Japanese
gardens. Kinkaku-ji is, if it is possible, even more
elegant and striking. It was built in the late 14th
century as a country villa but was converted to a
temple after the owner's death. In the same district,
Higashiyama, the Kiyomizu-dera is an amazing
structure, built on the side of a steep hill – it's wooden
platform gives spectacular views over the valley in
which the city sits.

The monuments of the World Heritage Site were
chosen because they each represented a particular
style of architecture and an era in the city's
development, but Kyoto has so much more to see:
there are some 1,700 Zen Buddist temples, 300 Shinto
shrines and assorted villas associated with the
imperial family. Kyoto's historic buildings and gardens
were once the source of inspiration and aspiration for
the rest of Japan. Their beauty is still a source of
inspiration for many people today.

*The stunning Golden
Pavilion*

Langkawi is famed for its white sandy beaches

Langkawi

Langkawi is the collective name for an archipelago of around 100 islands in the Andaman Sea, close to the north Malaysian coast. Only two are inhabited – Pulau Langkawi, the main island, and Pulau Tuba, and these are islands of rocky mountains, lush jungle and white sandy beaches lapped by green water.

'Langkawi' is sometimes translated as 'Land of Eagles', and you can still see white-bellied fish eagles here. However, the group is more popularly known as the 'Isles of Legends', and the best known of these is of Mahshiri, a beautiful woman falsely accused of adultery. It is said that when executed for this crime, she bled white blood, and cursed the islands for seven generations. Her tomb remains a major tourist attraction.

172

Curses notwithstanding, Langkawi has seen dramatic economic development in recent years: in 1987 it was designated a tax-free zone and later gained recognition as a UNESCO World Geopark. This combination has resulted in over two million visitors every year. Some of the best hotels in Malaysia are now situated here (this is not a budget destination!), mostly on the western side at Pantai Tenghah and Pantai Cenang, though the north coast is also developed. Despite this growth in tourism, the main town of Kuah retains its fishing heritage and relaxed lifestyle.

Government policy prohibiting beachfront development over coconut-tree-height is both commendable and in keeping with the up-market approach. Tax-free shopping aside, water sports are the major attraction here. Scuba diving and snorkelling are best within the Pulau Payar Marine Park. The interior of the island offers jungle trekking in one of the world's oldest rainforests, which is home to more than 200 bird species.

POPULATION:
60,000 (2005 estimate)
WHEN TO GO:
Year round
HOW TO GET THERE:
Boats from Penang, Kuala Perlis, Kuala Kedah and south Thailand. Flights from Kuala Lumpur, Georgetown, Ipoh, Singapore and Japan.
HIGHLIGHTS:
The cable car ride to the top of Gunung Mat Cinang. Lagend Lankawi Dalan Taman in Kuah – a 20-hectare (49-acre) theme park with giant sculptures illustrating some of the islands' many legends.
Crocodile Adventure on the north coast – Malaysia's largest crocodile farm, with over 1,500 saltwater crocs.
Telaga Tujuh – the 'Seven Pools' which you can slide down over the moss, preferably stopping before the water cascades over a cliff to form a 90 m (295 ft) waterfall.
YOU SHOULD KNOW:
The Galeria Perdaria contains a strange collection of over 10,000 items presented to the former Malaysian Prime Minister Dr Mahathir, who has been very influential in promoting Langkawi.

Hotels tend to be built using local architectural styles and materials.

Boracay Island

A typical tropical paradise in the Central Philippines, Boracay is just off the northwestern corner of the large island of Panay in the Visayas group. It rates as one of the country's top tourist destinations, but was a late starter – until the 1970s only the most clued-up of backpackers even knew the place existed.

The island is some 7 km (4 mi) long and extends to an area of some 10 sq km (4 sq mi). The reasons for coming are simple – sand and sea. The long main beach is on the west coast – and White Beach doesn't misrepresent itself. The sand is dazzling and the beach is sheltered from the prevailing wind in high season. This is the place for lazy loafing, with numerous beachfront facilities to cater for après-swim. Bulabog Beach on the east side is more athletically orientated, with kiteboarding and windsurfing on the menu. There are several other beaches for those who want to be different.

There are two distinct seasons on Boracay Island – Habagat and Amihan. They are associated respectively with, and vary in duration depending on the whims of, the global La Niña and El Niño weather patterns. Habagat (generally June to September) is hot and muggy with frequent heavy rain and unpredictable tropical storms. Amihan (usually October to May) sees little rainfall and moderate temperatures, with only the very occasional storm. The latter is very definitely high season.

Make no mistake – with nearly 400 beach resorts and the associated eating and drinking places, Boracay is an out-and-out tourist haven. But if you want to be marooned on a desert island for a week, 21st-century style, they don't come much better than this.

POPULATION:
12,000 (2000)

WHEN TO GO:
Amihan season (October to May) – more expensive, but worth it.

HOW TO GET THERE:
By internal flight to Godofredo P. Ramos Airport in nearby Caticlan, then boat from Caticlan Jetty to Cagban Beach on Boracay.

HIGHLIGHTS:
Traditional dragon-boat races featuring teams from all over the Philippines, held annually in April or May.

A self-sail tour of island waters in a hired *paraw* (canoe with two outriggers), or motorized *banca*.

Pitch and putt – actually a leisurely round on the world-class 18-hole par-72 course designed by top Aussie golfer Graham Marsh.

YOU SHOULD KNOW:
This isn't the ideal place to find peace and quiet – restaurants, clubs, bars and pubs sometimes keep going all night long.

One of Boracay Island's beautiful beaches.

175

POPULATION:
48,000 (2007)
WHEN TO GO:
Anytime, but it rains most in
November.
HOW TO GET THERE:
By ferry from Surat Thani, Ko
Pha Ngan or Ko Tao, or by
plane from Bangkok,
Phuket, Pattaya, Singapore,
Hong Kong or Kuala Lumpur.

Ko Samui

Ko Samui, in the Gulf of Thailand, lies some 80 km (50 mi) from the mainland town of Surat Thani. This was the first of the Gulf's islands to receive tourists – backpackers began arriving here about 30 years ago, moving on to Ko Pha Ngan and Ko Tao as the island became more developed. The building of an airport placed Samui firmly into the package holiday niche, leaving Pha Ngan to the partygoers and Tao to the divers.

Apart from tourism, the island is a huge coconut producer, harvesting some three million nuts per month, and palm trees and golden, sandy beaches are the hallmark of the place. At 15 km (9 mi) long and about the same in width, it's impossible not to notice that some of the development back from the beach is pretty nasty. Fortunately new construction cannot be higher than a coconut tree, although large hotel groups seem to get away with it.

Samui tries to cater for everyone, and the individual beaches that lie off the main coastal road do have their different atmospheres. Chaweng and Lamai are the most developed – some would

*A beach on Ko Samui
at sunset*

say ruined! Maenam and Bophut are quieter while Choeng Mon, in the north east, is really the classiest, with a few smart hotels round a pretty, tranquil bay.

This is a classic Thai holiday island. People come to swim, snorkel, and wander along the beaches in the daytime, stopping for a bite to eat, a massage, or to have beads braided into their hair. At night there are endless restaurants, bars and clubs to visit, some of which are home to Thai sex trade workers. Ko Samui really does go out of its way to provide tourists with whatever they fancy.

A couple enjoying the beautiful clear waters surrounding Ko Samui.

HIGHLIGHTS:
Bungy jumping at Chaweng beach.
Buffalo fighting.
Thai boxing.
The Butterfly Garden.
A day trip (at least) to the exquisite Ang Thong National Marine Park.

YOU SHOULD KNOW:
The first people to settle here were Chinese from Hainan Island, a mere 150 years ago. They were responsible for setting up the first coconut palm plantations.

The Islands of Phang-Nga Bay

POPULATION:
700 (2006 estimate)
WHEN TO GO:
December to May for the
best weather.
HOW TO GET THERE:
By boat from Phang-Nga
town, Phuket or Krabi.
HIGHLIGHTS:
Ko Panak, with its five
hidden *hongs*.
Khao Kien, with its ancient
rock paintings.
Ban Bor Tor, a long tunnel
filled with stalactites and
stalagmites.
YOU SHOULD KNOW:
These karst islands are the
perfect environment for
reptiles, in particular
water snakes.

Phang-Nga Bay is one of Thailand's most jaw-droppingly beautiful seascapes. Covering some 400 sq km (154 sq mi) tucked in between Phuket and Krabi, the bay, edged with mangrove forests, is home to hundreds of limestone karst formations. Some of these are tiny spires, some are large and bizarrely shaped, reaching up to 300 m (1,000 ft) in height, and all covered in tangled rain forest vegetation.

Formed some 12,000 years ago when the sea rose dramatically, flooding a limestone range that had already been eroded, some of the islands have been hollowed out by the forces of nature, leaving hidden, magical lagoons known as *hongs* in their centres. Invisible from the outside, the *hongs* are accessible by sea canoe, but it's only during certain tides that the channels beneath the seemingly impenetrable rock face are navigable. These secret lagoons are tidal, supporting their own ecosystems, while the

enclosing circle of cliff walls are covered with extraordinary vegetation, reminiscent of a prehistoric world.

The central area of the bay boasts fantastically sculpted karst islands, including the famous 'James Bond' island, where *The Man with the Golden Gun* was filmed. A stop here, of course, is part of every itinerary and the souvenir sellers are all there, waiting to pounce. Very few of these islands are inhabited, and even fewer have anywhere to stay.

Ko Panyi is an exception – a Muslim fishing village, mainly built on stilts, it teems with visitors during the daytime, but after they have gone it reverts to relative normality. Here you can rent your own sea canoe, and explore the bay at your leisure. It really is quite something – the cliffs are coloured with red and orange sponges close to the water line, and the scenery is awe-inspiring. Apart from rock climbing, most people come here for water-based activities – sea kayaking, sailing and, above all, fishing.

Phang Nga Bay

The Temple of Pura Ulun Danu Bratan

Bali

POPULATION:
3.2 million (2006)
WHEN TO GO:
Anytime, but the driest season is from May to September.
HOW TO GET THERE:
International or domestic flights to Denpasar or ferry from other Indonesian islands.
HIGHLIGHTS:
The beaches and beach life around the island.
The galleries and performance art in Ubud.
Tanah Lot, Bali's most picturesque temple.
Trekking round Tirta Gangga

Bali, the magical island of the gods, lives up to and beyond its reputation. Just 153 km (95 mi) wide and 112 km (69 mi) long, it is small enough to be driven around within a day. This is Indonesia's Hindu island, though like the other islands, animism exists beneath the surface, where art and beauty reign supreme. Three sacred volcanoes dominate the range straddling the north and east, providing fertile soil – local people say that if you put a bare stick in the earth, it will take root.

When Java's Islamic empire arose in the 16th century, the vanquished Hindus fled to Bali, reinforcing its culture but making an enemy. Over time Bali has been invaded by Java, Lombok, the Netherlands and Japan. In the 1960s thousands died when Mount Agung erupted, and 100,000 more were killed in retaliation for an unsuccessful communist coup against the government in Java. In 2002 and 2005, terrorist bombs killed and injured hundreds of both tourists and locals, but despite these tragedies Bali always recovers.

Beauty touches every aspect of daily life. The island is bursting with artists, wood carvers, musicians and dancers, with Ubud, in central Bali, the artistic heartland, having been home to many European artists since the 1920s. Tourism took off in the 1970s, but is contained in particular areas, leaving much of the island undisturbed. Here you can see classic scenes of brilliant green, terraced rice paddies, stone temples intricately carved with fabulous creatures, and *gamelan* orchestras accompanying gorgeously costumed dancers performing the Ramayana in the moonlight.

You can climb volcanoes, swim with dolphins, walk along near-empty beaches, admire exquisite offerings to the gods and watch colourful religious processions. Bali and its people are enchanting and completely irresistible.

and the water palace.
Shopping – you will be sorely tempted.
The Kecak (Monkey) Dance at sunset in Ulu Watu temple.

YOU SHOULD KNOW:
Negara, in south-west Bali, is famous for its bull races. Water buffalo, pulling small, decorative chariots and carrying elegantly dressed riders, dash hell for leather down the beach in front of a large, hugely appreciative audience.

A man carrying firewood and coconuts through rice paddies.

Mahé Island

WHEN TO GO:
All year round – the climate is evenly hot and humid. Even during the rainy season (January and February) there is plenty of sunshine.
HOW TO GET THERE:
Various international carriers fly to Mahé, including Air Seychelles – which also operates internal inter-island services.
HIGHLIGHTS:
The National Botanical Gardens on the outskirts of Victoria – a shady green oasis with a lovely orchid display.
Beau Vallon beach, the most popular on the island, where the action continues with good nightlife after dark.
The annual Creole Festival – a colourful (and noisy) event that takes place during the last week of October.
Victoria's Museum of History, full of exhibits and historic artefacts relating to the cultural and natural history of the Seychelles.
YOU SHOULD KNOW:
Although predominately Catholic, the Seychellois are a superstitious lot and many believe in old magic known as *gris*. But don't worry if you forget to tip – sorcery was officially outlawed in 1958!

Africa's least-populous sovereign state is the Republic of Seychelles, another of the Indian Ocean's fairly numerous island nations. Officially, there are over 150 islands in the Seychelles, consisting of a mix of granite and coral islands located 1,500 km (930 mi) to the east of the African mainland and 1,600 km (994 mi) to the north east of Madagascar. Other neighbours include Mauritius, Réunion, Zanzibar, Comoros, Mayotte and the Maldives. The Seychellois make good neighbours – they are often described as the world's friendliest people.

Mahé is the largest island, in the north of the archipelago. It contains the capital city of Victoria (no prizes for guessing that this was once a British colony) and has 90 per cent of the country's population. Settlement is concentrated in the north and east, while the south and west are largely occupied by the Baie Ternay Marine National Park and Port Launay Marine National Park. The island's high point, Morne Seychellois, is also a National Park that offers striking scenery and rewarding hiking opportunities. Visitors who merely pass through Mahé on the way to resort islands are missing something – the place is spectacular, with towering mountains, abundant tropical vegetation and beautiful beaches, mostly uncrowded...or, better still, empty.

One of the many glorious beaches on Mahé

Victoria is the world's smallest capital city, and its quaint streets and old harbour can easily be explored on foot. The clock tower is a replica of that housing Big Ben at London's Houses of Parliament. The market is open six days a week (excluding Sunday) and local crafts are on sale alongside a wide range of fruit, vegetables and fish. It's possible to take a boat tour of the St Anne Marine Park from Victoria Harbour, covering six offshore islands that include an important nesting site for hawksbill turtles.

The perfect place to indulge in a lazy afternoon?

WHAT IS IT?
A string of jewel-like coral islands, most of which are entirely devoted to tourism, which provide fabulous diving and snorkelling experiences.

HOW TO GET THERE:
By air to Male and then by boat to the other islands.

WHEN TO GO:
Hot all year round, December to April is the period of least rain.

NEAREST TOWN:
Male, the capital, is on the eponymous island.

The Maldives

The Maldive Islands are located 480 km (300 mi) south west of Cape Cormorin, on the southern tip of India. Consisting of 26 large atolls containing 1,190 islands, they run 648 km (405 mi) from north to south, and 130 km (81 mi) east to west, a double chain lying within the central area. Only 200 of the islands are inhabited and, of these, some 88 are exclusive holiday resorts.

The geomorphology of the Maldivian islands is unusual. An atoll is a coral formation surrounding a circular lagoon, but these lagoons, many of which are very large, are dotted with other, smaller, ring-shaped reefs, each surrounding its own sandy lagoon. These are known locally as *faros*, and this formation is known

as the Eye of the Maldives. Natural channels, allowing
the free movement of fish and currents between the
lagoons and the open sea, cut through each reef.

The islands are formed from coral sand, and are
very low lying, averaging no more than 2 m (6 ft 6 in),
with vegetation mainly consisting of coconut palms,
and mangroves. Just take a look, however, beneath the
surface of the turquoise sea and you will find glorious,
dazzling coral gardens teeming with multi-coloured fish
that are more curious than afraid of humans. The
diving and snorkelling here is
the main attraction, and the
exclusivity of many of its
resorts, which appeals to the
rich and famous.

Long term, the Maldives are
under threat. Climate change is
already adversely affecting the
coral, which can only thrive at
temperatures from 24 to 27 °C
(75 to 81 °F), and the natural
phenomena of El Niño and La
Niña have caused severe
bleaching to some of the
formations. Sea levels are also
rising, and although
preventative work is being
done, it seems that these fairy
tale coral islands will surely slip
beneath the surface of the sea
in the not too distant future.

*RIGHT: Heading for home
after an afternoon
spent snorkelling.*

*NEXT: A favourite pastime
in the Maldives – looking
at the sunset.*

Mauritius

Part of the Mascarene Islands, the Republic of Mauritius is off the coast of Africa in the Indian Ocean, 900 km (560 mi) east of Madagascar. The republic consists of five islands – St Brandon, Rodrigues, two Agalegas Islands and Mauritius itself. The latter was originally uninhabited, but the Dutch named the island and established a colony that was seized by the French in 1715. They renamed the place Ile de France and built a prosperous economy based on sugar. But the British took the island in 1810 and it reverted to the original name.

Independence was granted in 1968 and this Commonwealth country is a stable democracy with one of Africa's highest per capita incomes. This might be guessed by a visitor to Port Louis, who finds a sophisticated place with a cluster of high- and medium-rise buildings that might be mistaken from afar as the downtown area of a small American

Montagne du Rempart at sunset

Saga dancers

POPULATION:
1,288,000 (2009)
WHEN TO GO:
Temperature is high all year round, though trade winds keep down humidity. May to November are peak months, January and February are cyclone-prone.
HOW TO GET THERE:
By air from several departure points in Europe (especially France) and Africa.
HIGHLIGHTS:
Black River Gorges National Park – an area of outstanding natural beauty reached by the island's only mountain road.
Curepipe – in the centre of a lovely upland area, the place resembles an old English market town.
The Grand Bay Resort, for those who like some lively nightlife after a day on the beach.
The colourful Flacq Market in the east of the island for the best local produce and handicrafts.
Dutch ruins at Vieux Grand Port, the oldest settlement on the island, dating from the 17th century.
Chamarel – an extraordinary multi-coloured landscape made up of different volcanic ashes, culminating in a waterfall complex.
YOU SHOULD KNOW:
Mauritius was the only known habitat of that famous non-flying bird immortalized in the oh-so-sadly-true phrase 'dead as a dodo'.

city...were it not for its location beside the azure Indian Ocean, surrounded by lush tropical vegetation. Tourism has become an increasingly important sector of the economy, which had hitherto been based on sugar plantations and off-shore financial services.

The effort to attract visitors is proving successful, and might not even need the boost of a move to duty-free status. Mauritius is the most accessible island in the Indian Ocean, with wonderful beaches and crystal-clear waters. Important though these essential ingredients of every tropical holiday destination may be, Mauritius has something extra – friendly people and a vibrant cultural mix that will leave an indelible impression. There is a festival or fiesta practically every week and a tempting variety of ethnic cuisines. The place must be good – author Mark Twain remarked that Mauritius was made before heaven, and heaven was modelled on Mauritius.

ROMANTIC GETAWAYS IN
AFRICA

Rabat

Morocco's capital, Rabat, is a delightful surprise, its old quarter full of charm. Lying between the Atlantic coast and the estuary of the Bou Regreg River, it feels

The Bou Regreg River flows through Rabat.

pleasantly provincial and is less of a tourist destination than Marrakech or Fez. Divided between the old city and the new, it is easy to walk around – the sometimes tedious hassle that occurs elsewhere is less prevalent here.

Herbs, spices and nuts for sale at a souk in the Medina.

Some of Rabat's long and complex history is visible in its 12th century Almohad era walls and monuments, and its Kasbah and medina, which were both rebuilt by Andalucian pirates. Muslims of Moroccan extraction, these were refugees who were expelled from Christian Spain in 1610. Forming an anarchic republic here, their pirate fleet, the Sallée Rovers, captured merchant ships as far afield as the Caribbean during the next 200 years. In 1912, when the French formed a Protectorate here, they built the new town outside the walls, and re-established the city as their capital, which King Mohammed V elected to retain on gaining Moroccan independence in 1956.

The fortified Kasbah is like a Spanish village, light and airy, all the houses are sparkling white with blue paintwork. Enclosed by huge walls, one enters through the Oudaia Gate, one of the finest of Moorish gates, built in 1195. Visit the 17th century Royal Palace, with its Museum of Moroccan Arts and enjoy the beautiful Andalucian gardens. A viewing platform at the northern end of the Kasbah gives splendid views over the harbour and the ocean.

The medina, also walled, is more orderly than most. Wander through the clean, narrow, residential streets, stone houses with studded wooden doors rising on either side. Turn a corner and find a mass of busy little shops and stalls, working craftsmen and cafés. The new town, with its parks and tree-lined streets, is obviously French, and contains all the embassies and government buildings.

Taroudant

An ideal base for the exploration of the Souss Valley and western High Atlas, Taroudant is known for its bustling market and fresh produce. A mixture of Arabic and Tashelhit Berber languages can be heard as you stroll through the town's recently restored salmon-coloured walls.

As you head towards the market you'll weave through crowds of men on bicycles with fresh bundles of coriander in their baskets, fish mongers, men tanning leather, shining brass pans or carving wood. The enticing smells of lavender, thyme, saffron and mint waft through the hazy sunshine, as you stop to admire the Grand Mosque with its yellow minaret and teal-green houndstooth tiling.

On a clear day, the snowy peaks of the Djebel Toubkal can be seen hovering in the distance past the

POPULATION:
63,000 (2004)
WHERE IS IT?
85 km (51 mi) east of Agadir, 223 km (134 mi) south-west of Marrakesh.
DON'T MISS:
The markets enjoying the sights and smells of the relaxed town.
WHAT TO BUY:
The area is known for its olive oil. Carpets, pottery, wooden boxes, silver, saffron and lavender are also worth picking up.

A terraced landscape in Taroudant

gates of the Kasbah. The native women, the Roudani,
can be seen in the early evenings chatting in lines
around the ramparts in their colourful clothes. They
look, and often sound, like an exotic species of bird as
they wander around gossiping and laughing.

Stop at one of the many reasonably priced cafés and enjoy a snack as you watch daily life unfold, take a *calèche*, (a horse-drawn carriage), around the city and watch the fading light of sunset highlight the olive trees surrounding the town.

The city walls and ramparts in Taroudant with the Atlas Mountains behind the city.

Cape Verde Islands

POPULATION:
420,979 (2006)

WHEN TO GO:
October and November when the land is green after the rains, and before the winds pick up in December.

HOW TO GET THERE:
International flights to Sal and Santiago.
Sporadic ferry services from Dakar and Las Palmas.

HIGHLIGHTS:
Mindelo Carnaval on São Vicente in February – with Rio-style floats and costumes.
Taking in the lively port city of Mindelo on São Vicente.
The lovely town of Vila Nova Sintra on Brava.
Vila de Ribeira Grande on Santo Antao – the first European town in the tropics.

The port city of Mindelo on São Vicente

Tipping off the African map, the Cape Verde Islands would appear to sit more happily with the Azores, or even the Canary Islands. Composed of nine main islands in two groups – the Windwards and the Leewards – six are volcanic and shapely, while three are sandy and flat. This is no tropical paradise, yet despite the hassle of getting here the islands are well worth the trek.

The Portuguese arrived here in 1460 and made the islands part of the Portuguese empire. Cape Verde became an important watering station for passing ships, then a sugar cane plantation site, and later a major hub of the transatlantic slave trade. In 1975, Cape Verde gained independence from Portugal.

With jumbled African and Portuguese roots, Cape Verdeans certainly know how to make music and dance – samba and salsa sprinkled with African tribal sounds. The soft *morna* lament gives way to the sensual, upbeat *coladeira* and *batuque* dance, and love songs unfurl in Cape Verdean Creole. The official language may be Portuguese, but Creole is favoured colloquially.

The first port of call is often Praia on Santiago Island –

Cape Verde's capital. The beaches are fine and white and the mountains impressive, but more importantly it forms the perfect springboard for island hopping. Brava is the smallest inhabited island, the hardest to reach but also the most beautiful. On brooding Fogo there is fine walking, and hikes up into the old volcano crater. There is a good deal of rivalry and many cultural differences between islands – right down to the way the women tie their headscarves.

This small nation lacks resources and has suffered severe droughts. Over the centuries, disastrous famines have continually rocked the lives of the islanders, yet their spirit remains alive and contagious.

Fontainhas Village

DON'T MISS:
Breakfast on *cachupa* – a delicious bean dish.
Island hopping by ferry – discovering the islands' delights for yourself.
YOU SHOULD KNOW:
The easiest place to get a visa is in Lisbon, or by going through a specialist travel company. In West Africa, the only consulate is in Dakar, Senegal – once you have found it, getting a visa should be easy.

The tranquil village of Shela

Lamu Island

Part of the Lamu Archipelago in the Indian Ocean close to the northern coast of Kenya, Lamu Island is surrounded by long, white sandy beaches framed by rolling dunes, as unspoiled today as they were when the island was first settled in the 14th century.

A port was founded on the island by Arab traders, who built the Pwani Mosque. The port prospered on the export of timber, ivory and amber, and soon became a major centre for the slave trade. After defeating nearby Pate Island in the 19th century, Lamu became a major local power. After the abolition of slavery in 1873, however, the island's economy suffered and has never

made a come back. Today, tourism is an important source of income here.

Lamu town, the largest settlement on the island, was founded in the 14th century and contains many fine examples of Swahili architecture. The old town is designated a World Heritage Site as the oldest and best-preserved Swahili settlement in East Africa. With the simple lines of its architecture, built in coral and mangrove wood and featuring porches and rooftop patios, the town has managed to retain its distinctive character and charm. Donkeys wander through the narrow labyrinthine streets as there are no motorized vehicles on this idyllic island.

There are several museums in town, including the Lamu Museum which displays the island's ceremonial horn, and another museum dedicated to Swahili culture. Also worth a visit is Lamu Fort, built on the seafront by the Sultan of Pate in the early 17th century to protect members of his unpopular government. The Riyadha Mosque was built in 1900 and soon became one of the most prestigious centres for Islamic studies in Eastern Africa. The mosque is the centre for the annual Maulidi Festival which attracts pilgrims from all over Africa.

The most spectacular beaches on the island are those around Shela, a village about 3.2 km (2 mi) from Lamu town, with their clean white sand and traditional dhows. The area was unfortunately damaged in 2004 during the tsunami caused by the Indian Ocean earthquake, but it is still a lovely place to while away the day.

WHEN TO GO:
December to January
HOW TO GET THERE:
Fly from Mombasa or Nairobi, or take a ferry from Mokowe on the mainland or Manda Island.
HIGHLIGHTS:
Just chilling out – as there are no cars, this is a very peaceful place with just the sound of braying donkeys and palm trees rustling in the breeze. Leave the mobile phone and laptop at home and enjoy the tranquillity.
The Lamu Museum – housed in a building once occupied by Jack Haggard, Queen Victoria's consul. There are displays on Swahili culture, including a reconstructed Swahili house and relics from Takwa. Here the ceremonial horn of the island is on display.
The seafront restaurants in Lamu town – enjoy very fresh seafood at reasonable prices.
The donkey sanctuary in northern Lamu – set up to protect the 2,200 working donkeys on the island and ensure their well-being.
YOU SHOULD KNOW:
Lamu is strictly Islamic so be sensitive as to how you dress.

Zanzibar

Located 35 km (22 miles) from the coast of Tanzania in the Indian Ocean is Zanzibar, boasting white sand beaches lined with palm trees, native forests and an abundance of coral reefs perfect for snorkelling and diving. Today it offers a tropical paradise for holidaymakers, but this low-lying coral island has a chequered history of foreign occupation, intensive commerce and slavery.

The island was first inhabited by the Hadimu and

Watching the sunset.

POPULATION:
1,070,000 (2004)
WHEN TO GO:
June to October.
HOW TO GET THERE:
Fly to Zanzibar International Airport or by ferry from Dar es Salaam.
HIGHLIGHTS:
The beaches – the island has many lovely beaches for sunbathing and swimming. The East Beaches are popular as the sand is brilliant white, and the warm waters are deep blue. The scuba diving is good here, with plentiful corals and rich marine life. Swim with the dolphins or arrange a ride in a local's dhow.
Stone Town – explore the lovely buildings, like the House of Wonders and the Arab Fort. Arrange a walking tour with a local guide who can explain some of the fascinating history. Jozani Park – this beautiful forest has excellent nature trails, featuring some very exotic (and large) trees. See the Red Colobus Monkeys which are native to the island but now nearly extinct. They are curious and playful and will pose for a photograph.
Spice tours – these enjoyable organized tours explain how the different spices grow, allowing you to tour the beautiful plantations of cardamom, ginger, cloves, nutmeg and saffron, and sample some luscious tropical fruits.
YOU SHOULD KNOW:
Zanzibar was the last place to abolish the slave trade.

204

Tumbatu tribes who came here from Africa. In the 10th century, Persian merchants arrived, brought to the island by monsoon winds as they sailed through the Indian Ocean. As they needed the monsoon winds to take them home again, they had to stay on the island for months at a time. They eventually decided to build permanent settlements on Zanzibar, and it soon became a centre for trade in its own right. This busy hub was influenced by the merchants who passed through, with Arabs, Indians, Chinese, Portuguese, Dutch and British leaving their mark here and blending together to create a unique culture.

Shirazi Persians and Omani Arabs settled on the island and ruled the Sultanate, which is why there is such a strong Arab influence evident today. Stone Town, the centre of the old city, has changed little in the last 200 years with its mosques, busy bazaars and grand Arab houses with their ornamental carved wooden doors studded with brass. The Indian influence can be found in the coloured glasswork and decorative balconies of many of the buildings, while the British left some staid colonial houses in the wealthier parts of town.

Today the economy is based on tourism, although fishing is still a major occupation. The island also exports many different types of spices, as well as cocoa and coconuts.

As well as the beaches and beautiful architecture, the

island is also home to abundant wildlife, including red colobus and blue monkeys, which can be observed in Jozani Park, a large area of mature native forest which is now protected. There are also many other types of mammals here, including red-bellied squirrels and sun squirrels, and over 200 species of birds. Zanzibar is also a good place to see turtles, including the green turtle and the hawksbill turtle, which can be seen laying their eggs on the beaches near the lighthouse at Ras Ngunwi. Whale watching is also popular here, with humpback whales migrating through the channel in spring and then again in September. Long-snouted spinner dolphins and bottlenose dolphins are also favourites in these waters and it is possible to swim with them if you join an organized tour.

Two dhows sail past Stone Town.

Victoria Falls

Known to the people of the Kololo tribe who lived in the area in the nineteenth century as 'Mosi-oa-Tunya' - 'the Smoke that Thunders', Victoria Falls is one of nature's greatest spectacles. The spray above it can be seen from almost 65 km (40 mi) away. The River Zambezi flows through a shallow valley across a flat basalt plateau for

miles, but in some places, cracks in the basalt exposed the weaker sandstone below and the water was able to force a way through and begin to erode it. The 8 km (5 mi) of steep-sided gorges the Zambezi cuts through here represent hundreds of thousands of years of erosion.

Victoria Falls is neither the highest nor the broadest waterfall on earth, but with a single drop of 108 m (360 ft) and a width of 1.7 km (1 mi), it is claimed to be the

Victoria Falls are on the border of Zambia and Zimbabwe.

WHAT IS IT?
One of the largest waterfalls
on earth, set in a
spectacular gorge.
HOW TO GET THERE:
By air to Livingstone or
Victoria Falls, by road or rail
from Lusaka or by rail from
South Africa, then by car.
WHEN TO GO:
Winter, when the flood is
not at its peak but the falls
are not obscured by spray.
NEAREST TOWN:
Livingstone 10 km (6 mi)
DON'T MISS:
A plane ride over the falls.

*A spectacular view
along the narrow gorge*

single largest falling sheet of water. At the peak of the
rainy season, more than 546 cu m (2.5 million gallons)
spill over the falls per minute.

Because the gorge is so narrow, it is simple for
visitors to get a spectacular view of the thundering
waters from as little as 60 m (200 ft) away, if they are
prepared both to brave the path along the opposite edge
and to get very, very wet. The Knife-Edge Bridge affords
views of the main falls, the Boiling Pot and the Eastern
Cataract, while the Lookout Tree and Victoria Falls
Bridge give panoramic views of the falls and gorge.

At the height of the river's spate in March to May, a
plane ride along the gorge and above the falls makes an
exhilarating experience and an amazing way to see one
of nature's best wonders.

Kalahari Desert and Okavango Delta

The Kalahari Desert, which spreads over 930,000 sq km (360,000 sq mi) of Botswana, South Africa and Namibia, is a semi-arid land subject to summer rainfall that provides grazing. The only permanent river in this red-brown, dusty land is the Okavango, which runs south-east from the highlands of Angola and drains into the Okavango Delta in the north-west of the Kalahari, creating an area full of spectacular wildlife. The highlight is the Moremi Wildlife Reserve. Seasonal rainfall in the Angolan highlands leads the delta to flood in the north in mid-summer (November to December) and in the south in mid-winter (May to June), giving rise to a constantly changing landscape.

Animals that inhabit the reserves in the Kalahari include several species of antelope, brown hyenas, lions, African wild dogs, cheetahs and meerkats. Among the spectacles of this arid region are the massive communal nests of weaver birds, which drape the acacia trees.

The delta itself is home to such large mammals as African elephants, African buffalo, hippos, and black and

WHAT IS IT?
A wildlife heaven set in the middle of a giant desert.
HOW TO GET THERE:
By air to Maun, Botswana, then overland.
WHEN TO GO:
May to October.
NEAREST TOWN:
Maun 80 km (50 mi) from the Moremi Wildlife Reserve
DON'T MISS
A canoe trip on the river.

Night-blooming water lilies in a lagoon in the Okavango Delta.

white rhinos. Giraffes, blue wildebeest, zebras, warthogs and chacma baboons are also here, as well as species of antelope such as lechwe, topi and greater kudu. Predators and scavengers here include lions, leopards, cheetahs, hyenas and wild dogs and the waters harbour Nile crocodiles and water monitors. More than 450 species of birds have been seen here, including crested cranes and African fish eagles.

A visit to this beautiful, lush landscape, set within the surrounding desert, is an experience that will not easily be forgotten.

A fisherman in the Okavango Delta at sunset

Little Namaqualand

*Skilpad Flower Reserve
with Pigroot flowers
in the foreground*

Little Namaqualand is a sunburned, semi-arid region
of some 60,000 sq km (23,000 sq mi) that lies south of
the Orange River, in South Africa's Northern Cape
Province. It is a winter-rainfall desert, with much of
the area receiving less than 150 mm (6 in) of rain
each year.

Along its rugged western shores the cold Atlantic
breakers pound, and sea mists frequently roll in,
gripping the region in a clammy embrace. Alluvial
diamonds have been found on this coast, but these
crystalline beauties are no match for the true gems of
Namaqualand – its flowers.

For although this region is dry and almost lifeless
for nine months of the year, with the spring comes a
transformation that is as beautiful as it is remarkable.
Late winter rains awake the life that is lying just
beneath the surface, and all at once the land is awash
in a sea of colour. Flowers of every hue imaginable,

WHAT IS IT?
A desert that bursts into
bloom each spring.
HOW TO GET THERE:
By road up the N7 from
Cape Town.
WHEN TO GO:
July to October.
NEAREST TOWN:
Springbok is the region's
main town.
DON'T MISS:
The Geogap Nature Reserve
in Springbok.
YOU SHOULD KNOW:
During the spring you can
telephone 'flower hotlines'
to discover where the best
blooms are. The area
becomes very busy when
the flowers are in bloom.

211

Spring flowers in Namaqualand

almost simultaneously burst into bloom creating a spectacle that is in every sense of the word, wonderful.

Most of the flowers are various species of daisy, but home to some 3,000 species – nearly half of which are found nowhere else – Namaqualand is truly a plant-lover's paradise. Although most of the plants here are ground hugging, two larger ones worth searching out are the halfmens and the quiver tree. The rare halfmens – or half-person – is a triffid-like succulent that bends to face the sun as it grows. Taller still is the remarkable quiver tree, so named because Bushmen use its branches to make quivers for their arrows. This

distinctive plant is often the tallest plant around, and as a result is popular with birds. Sugarbirds feed on the flowers, weaverbirds nest in its branches and hawks use it as a welcome vantage point from which to spy prey.

For those visitors who arrive in Namaqualand 'out of season' this unique landscape still has much to offer. Aside from the uncountable number of succulents, the desert itself also possesses a special beauty, with its shattered landscape of billion-year-old granite and huge over-arching skies that at night twinkle with stars as bright as any earthly diamond.

The Namib Desert

Hot air ballooning in Namib Naukluft Park

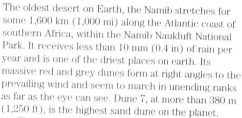

The oldest desert on Earth, the Namib stretches for some 1,600 km (1,000 mi) along the Atlantic coast of southern Africa, within the Namib Naukluft National Park. It receives less than 10 mm (0.4 in) of rain per year and is one of the driest places on earth. Its massive red and grey dunes form at right angles to the prevailing wind and seem to march in unending ranks as far as the eye can see. Dune 7, at more than 380 m (1,250 ft), is the highest sand dune on the planet.

The interaction between the dry air of the desert and moisture-laden air over the sea causes immense fogs to form, and to the north lies the Skeleton Coast, the final resting place of many ships lost in the fog and unable to escape the strong currents.

For many of the animals in the desert, the fog is a lifeline, bringing extra moisture to this arid landscape, allowing insects and small reptiles to survive. There is a surprising variety of wildlife here, with 45 species of lizards and 200 types of beetles, as well as wasps and spiders. Reptiles here include geckos and sidewinder snakes, which make a distinctive pattern of waves in the sand as they move. Birds that breed here include sand grouse and ostrich, while the mammals are represented by baboons.

From the top of one of these dunes, sunrise and sunset are spectacular events, as the dunes are 'painted' in different colours with the changing light. At the coast, the sight of the swollen sun slipping below the sea is an added bonus.

RIGHT: Sand dunes in Namib Naukluft National Park

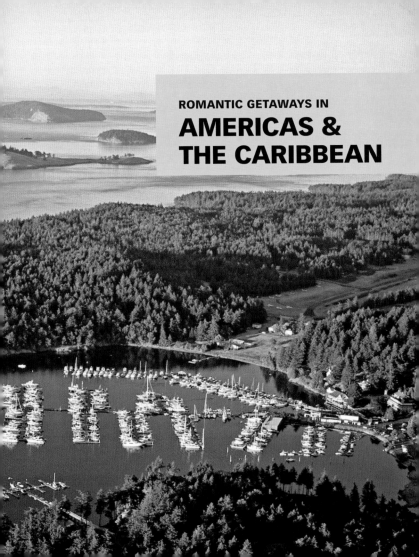

ROMANTIC GETAWAYS IN
AMERICAS &
THE CARIBBEAN

Cape Breton Island

Nova Scotia's Cape Breton has an untamed beauty that makes for some of the most impressive scenery in North America. Covering 10,311 sq km (3,981 sq mi), the island is a wonderful mixture of rocky shores, rolling pasture, barren headlands, woodland, mountains and plateaux.

The Cape Breton Highlands, an extension of the Appalachian Mountain chain and a national park

since 1936, dominate the north part of the island. The famous Cabot Trail Scenic Highway, one of the most spectacular scenic drives in Canada, winds through nearly 300 km (185 mi) of this ruggedly beautiful countryside.

Comprehension of the people of Cape Breton Island is not possible without some knowledge of its earliest settlers. Cape Bretoners today reflect the resolve of those pioneers – whether their roots are Mi'kmaq, Acadian, Scottish, Irish or Black Loyalist.

The Island has shaped them just as they struggled to shape the island. Since then settlers have arrived from all over the world and have made their own distinct contributions.

The largest town, Sydney, still bears the scars of a failed industrial past but outside of the immediate area, the theme of the island is heritage mixed with outstanding natural beauty. Fortress Louisbourg faithfully recreates the French military might of the early 18th century, pioneer cottages line the north shore of the imposing Bras d'Or Lake and the island's most northerly point, Meat Cove, offers incredibly spectacular, unspoilt ocean views.

Accommodation on Cape Breton is limited, so booking in advance is recommended, and as the public transport is poor, driving is your only real option to explore this wonderful land.

POPULATION:
150,000 (2004)
WHEN TO GO:
June to August is the best time but even then the weather is notoriously unpredictable. Though colder, September to early November offers a spectacular vista of flaming leaf colours.
HOW TO GET THERE:
By road-bridge from mainland Nova Scotia or by air to Sydney which has an international airport.
HIGHLIGHTS:
Hiking around Fortress Louisbourg.
Nature watching on Lake Ainslee.
Driving around the Cabot Trail Highway.
Fishing for salmon on the Margaree River.
Cheticamp – the largest Acadian community in Nova Scotia.
The Celtic Colours Festival in early October – a celebration of fiddle playing.
YOU SHOULD KNOW:
Much beloved by the inventor of the telephone, Alexander Graham Bell, Cape Breton was at the centre of a communications mix-up when an English couple made an online booking to go to Sydney, Australia only to find themselves flown to Sydney, Canada.

A couple enjoying the views from the Cabot Trail.

219

Quebec City

One of the oldest cities in North America, Quebec City is the capital of the province of the same name and in Vieux-Quebec has the only surviving walled city in the Americas north of Mexico. The historic district of Quebec was designated a UNESCO World Heritage Site in 1985 for its cultural and historical significance. Its twin areas – Basse-Ville and Haute-Ville – surround the Château Frontenac. In Haute-Ville, you will find narrow lanes running between grey, high-walled houses reminiscent of a medieval French city, while lower down Cap Diamant Basse-Ville – the site of the original settlement – is home to a lively café culture and boutique shops.

The Château Frontenac is one of the city's dominant landmarks: this large hotel on the Cap Diamant is a model Loire château. The Basilica of Notre-Dame is also very French in feel. Another building left from colonial times is the Haute-Ville's Citadelle, a star-shaped complex of military fortifications. In Basse-Ville you will find the church of Notre-Dame des Victoires. One of the areas best-known attractions is the Musée de la Civilisation.

There is a wide range of museums that cover the history and culture of the region, among them the Musée de Quebec in the Parc des Champs-de Bataille, which has a fanstastic art collection. The park is the site of the battle that ended the rule of the French in North America and holds free concerts in summer.

At the other end of the year the Quebecois cheer themselves up with the biggest winter carnival in the world, which features a talking snowman called Bonhomme, who inhabits the Snow Palace and presides over horse-drawn sleigh rides, the International Canoe Race across the part-frozen St Lawrence River, dogsled races, parades and the International Snow Sculpture Event. What better way could there be to chase the winter blues away?

Right: Shoppers walking along a snow-covered street.

Next: The Château Frontenac is the city's dominant landmark.

Queen Charlotte Islands

WHAT ARE THEY?
An archipelago of 1,884 islands, with snow-topped mountains and fiords that plunge into the sea, mist-enshrouded forests and windswept sandy beaches. They are sometimes referred to as the Galapagos Islands of the North.

WHERE ARE THEY?
The Queen Charlottes are located in British Columbia, Canada, west of the northern BC town of Prince Rupert. Two islands, Graham Island in the north and Moresby Island in the south, make up the majority of the land mass.

HOW TO GET THERE:
The main airport for the islands is at Sandspit.

HIGHLIGHTS:
There are countless beaches, streams, fishing holes, coves and abandoned Indian villages to explore. Many unique subspecies of flora and fauna share these islands with the residents.

YOU SHOULD KNOW:
The Haida people refer to the islands as *Haida Gwaii* – islands of the people or *Xhaaidlagha Gwaayaai* – Islands at the Boundary of the World.
According to Haida legend, Haida Gwaii is the place where time began.

Arguably one of the most beautiful and diverse landscapes in the world, the Queen Charlotte Islands have such thriving and abundant flora and fauna that they are sometimes called the 'Galapagos of the North'.

The scenery of the 1,884 islands of the archipelago is stunning. The seven largest islands, peaks of a submerged mountain chain, are Langara, Graham, Moresby, Louise, Lyell, Burnaby and Kunghit islands. Just 2 or 3 km (1.2–2 mi) offshore, the continental shelf falls away dramatically to the immense depths of the Pacific Ocean, making this the most active earthquake area in Canada and landslides are common.

Haida Gwaii has been home to the Haida people for at least 7,000 years. In 1774, Juan Perez was the first European to reach this isolated paradise. Fur traders followed, creating a major impact on the Haida as Europeans arrived *en masse* to exploit the abundant resources. In 1787, the islands were renamed after Lord Howe's flagship, HMS *Queen Charlotte*, in honour of Queen Charlotte, wife of King George III.

The islands retain their wild peace and have a rich cultural history. The Haida earn their living traditionally, the main industries being mining, logging and commercial fishing. Tourist activities include sport fishing, hiking, camping, kayaking and whalewatching.

Graham Island is the most accessible and populated of the islands, and is where the majority of the Haida communities reside. The adjacent islands great for exploring the Haida culture include: Skidegate, on the shores of Rooney Bay, the cultural centre of the area where you can see artefacts and local art; Tlell, home to an artistic collective, the heart of the art community and the Haida's administrative seat; Old Masset, home to native carvers; and the remote and rugged Langara Island, at the north-west tip of the archipelago, with its ancient rainforest, an impressive seabird colony and a restored 1913 lighthouse.

Other places to explore are the logging and fishing village of Port Clements, where you can see the giant trees of the temperate rainforest and North Beach in

Naikoon Provincial Park where, the Haida believe, the raven first brought people into the world by coaxing them out of a clam shell.

The vast rugged coastline of Rennell Sound, bordered by the snow-capped Queen Charlotte Mountains, offers scenic beaches, great hiking, fishing and kayaking and Louise Island, where you can view one of the largest displays of ancient totem poles in these spiritual islands.

A totem pole stands at the site of the Haida Museum and Cultural Center in Skidegate.

225

San Francisco

POPULATION:
4,204,000 (2008)
WHEN TO GO:
Any time of year.
DON'T MISS:
The 49-mile Drive.
Colt Tower.
Pier 39.
The drive across the bay to
Oakland.
YOU SHOULD KNOW:
Don't call it Frisco: the
locals don't like it.
DON'T MISS:
Lombard Street – 'the
crookedest street in
the world'.
Golden Gate Bridge.
A tour of Alcatraz.
A day trip to the wineries in
Napa and Sonoma, with
opportunites for tastings.

Whatever image you have of San Francisco before you get here, you will find that it doesn't match up to the reality. Golden Gate Bridge is just as spectacular as you thought it would be, the hills are as steep as you imagined and, yes, there are still tie-dyed teenagers looking to find themselves around Haight-Ashbury. It's no surprise that San Francisco is always among the top tourist destinations in the world.

Despite being densely populated, the city's location on the waterfront, parks and the way that the hills ensure you can never see more than a few blocks make it seem more like a small town rather than the centre of a metropolis of more than 4 million people.

Among the highlights of a trip here is the obligatory visit to Alcatraz Island's 'inescapable' prison, as well as a drive across the Golden Gate Bridge, a trip that must be reserved for a sunny day. Golden Gate Park is home to the M.H. de Young Museum and one of the best botanical gardens in the world, as well as a great place for a picnic. It's also home to a herd of bison.

Neighbourhoods that are worth seeking out include North Beach (also known as Little Italy) and Chinatown. The Castro, is home to a thriving café culture and plenty of small art galleries, as well as being one of the focal areas for the city's gay population.

Fisherman's Wharf is the place to go for the regional speciality, Dungeness crabs, which you can eat while watching the sea lions lazing around in the sunshine.

The Museum of Modern Art is housed in an amazing building in South of Market, while the Palace of Fine Arts is in Pacific Heights, overlooking the Golden Gate and has a popular science museum. The Palace of the Legion of Honour in Lincoln Park has mainly European paintings. Other museums explore the African Diaspora, San Francisco's own history, craft and folk art, Mexican, Chinese and Jewish culture, among many other things.

A ride on the cable cars is a must – take a trip from Fisherman's Wharf or Union Square up to Nob Hill, home to the rich. It's also worth the trip to see the Grace Cathedral.

San Francisco has some of the best in sightseeing, dining, culture, history and scenery, and truly does have something to offer everyone.

BELOW: Russian Hill and San Francisco Bay

NEXT: Golden Gate Bridge at night

Charleston

On the Atlantic coast of
South Carolina, Charleston
was originally named after
Charles II, some four years
afer his restoration to the
thrones of England and
Scotland. It was originally a
walled city, and was home
to two forts famous for their
pivotal roles in America's
history: Fort Moultrie
withstood the British in the
Revolutionary Wars and
Fort Sumter is thought to be
the location of the first shot
of the American Civil War.
The only part of the original
walls to remain is the
Powder Magazine. Its site on
a peninsula between the
Ashley and Cooper rivers
made it an ideal location for
a defence and the blockade
of its port was a pivotal – if
not always successful – part
of the North's strategy
during the American Civil
War because it was a vital
source of revenue for the
South. The port is still
among the largest and busiest in the world.

The downtown area is home to the central business
district and many cultural and historic sites. The revenue
from surrounding plantations made the city rich and the
surviving buildings from this era include St Michael's
Episcopal Church, the Old Exchange and Customs

One of the many grand houses in Charleston

House (scene of the ratification of the US Constitution in 1788), the City Hall and the County Court House. There are also many pretty houses in 'historic Charleston', the epitome of Southern colonial charm, with grand houses on tree-lined streets that drip with Spanish moss. Rainbow Row, by the waterfront, has a collection of

pastel-coloured historic homes.

In some ways similar to New Orleans, Charleston's culture is a mixture of French, West African and traditional southern American. The French influence can be seen in the dainty red-and-white Huguenot church.

The area's plantation past can be seen in the Boone Hall and Magnolia Plantations, Drayton Hall and Middleton Place, while the Charleston Museum was the first museum on the American continent and the Gibbes Museum is home to more than 10,000 works of art. There are many other museums and historical attractions lurking around almost every corner. Each district of the city has its own unique character and charm with dozens of gardens and parks to chill out in and plenty of marinas.

Round porches of a mansion in the East Battery district of Charleston

232

Savannah

One of the most beautiful cities in the Americas, Savannah is the epitome of what the United States' deep south ought to look like. It is one of the most historically significant places in America. It retains significant numbers of buildings that date back to the early and mid-19th century and beyond, with typical verandahs and balconies dripping with Spanish moss and surrounded by lush oak and tropical woodland. It is also known for the typical laid-back southern charm of its inhabitants.

The settlement was founded in 1733 by General James Edward Oglethorpe and a group of 120 like-minded individuals and it became the capital of the thirteenth British colony in America, Georgia.

Sadly, Savannah's wealth came on the back of the slave trade – through both the import of slaves and the export of cotton, deerskin and rice.

POPULATION:
334,000 (2008)
WHEN TO GO:
Any time of year.
DON'T MISS:
Forsyth Park – home to Forsyth Fountain; a large, ornate, two-tiered cast iron icon of Savannah.
The Savannah Film Festival.
The Second African Baptist Church on Greene Square.
Johnson Square – the first and largest square in the city.
The jazz and blues clubs.
The Telfair Museum of Art.
YOU SHOULD KNOW:
Eli Whitney invented the cotton gin near here in 1793.
The cotton gin is the machine that separates the cotton fibres from the seeds.

A row of trees covered in Spanish Moss

The historic area of the city has been declared a National Historic Landmark. Oglethorpe had laid it out in a grid form, envisaging broad streets interspersed with parks and shaded public squares, of which the majority survive to this day. In the 19th century, the growth, production and export of cotton became increasingly important to the southern parts of America and Savannah became one of the main centres of the industry.

Other early buildings that survive, if in a restored condition, include the Herb House, the oldest building to survive in Georgia, dating back to the year after the colony was founded, the Pirates' House from the 1750s and the Pink House from the 1780s, as well as the Owens-Thomas House, Wormsloe Plantation, and the Sorrel Weed House.

Unlike so many other southern cities, much of the historic area of Savannah survived the Civil War, chiefly because General Sherman was so impressed by its beauty he decided to spare it. Many freed slaves remained in the area, forming one of the most significant African-American communities in the country.

The middle of the 20th century was not so kind to the historic areas, and after various important buildings were demolished, the Historic Savannah Foundation was set upin order to stop the awful destruction, and eventually led to the city's emergence as a tourist destination.

The city is not just about the historic district: the City Market and the River Street area are filled with popular shops and restaurants while Tybee Island is a popular beach resort. Fort Jackson was important during the Civil War and the Laurel Grove and Bonaventure cemeteries are   worth visiting.

A wonderful example of the architecture to be found in Savannah

The Florida Keys

The Florida Keys are one of America's biggest tourist attractions. This subtropical archipelago is made up of 1,700 islands which begin at the south-eastern tip of Florida and extend in a gentle arc south-west and

236

A pier on Key Largo

then west to Key West, the furthest of the inhabited islands, and on to the uninhabited Dry Tortugas, only 145km (90 mi) from Cuba.

'Key' is a corruption of the Spanish *cayo*, meaning small island. For many years, Key West was the largest town in Florida, grown wealthy on plundering the many ships wrecked on the nearby rocks and reefs.

WHEN TO GO:
November to May.
HOW TO GET THERE:
Fly to Key West or Marathon
airports, or drive via the
scenic
Overseas Highway.
HIGHLIGHTS:
Conch fritters followed by
Key Lime Pie.
The lovely guest houses
with wrap-around porches
in Key West.
The tropical hospitality of
Jimmy Buffet's famed
'Margaritaville' – located on
Duval Street, Key West, this
laid-back bar serves fine
local food and drinks to the
sound of live music.
Relax on one of the fabulous
beaches, go sport fishing,
have a romantic seaside
meal, swim with dolphins,
look for manatees.
The Ernest Hemmingway
Home and Museum – visit
the house in Old Town, Key
West, where the famous
author lived and wrote for
ten years. Relive
Hemmingway's lifestyle at
one of his favourite
watering holes after
your visit.
PrideFest – this week-long
festival takes place in early
June to celebrate Key
West's Gay and Lesbian
community.
YOU SHOULD KNOW:
Key West has long been
noted as a gay vacation
destination, and is home to
the United States' first Gay
and Lesbian Chamber of
Commerce.

This isolated outpost was well placed for trade with Cuba, and was on the main trade route from New Orleans. Eventually, better navigation led to fewer shipwrecks, and Key West went into a decline in the late 19th century.

The Keys were long accessible only by water. This changed when Henry Flagler built his Overseas Railway in the early 20th century. Flagler extended his Florida East Coast Railway down to Key West using a series of over-sea railroad trestles, a bold and ambitious project for the time it was built. The Labor Day hurricane hit the Keys in 1935, however, with wind speeds of up to 200 miles per hour, and put paid to the Overseas Railway. The damaged tracks were never rebuilt, but the Overseas Highway (an extension of US Highway 1) replaced the railway as the main transportation route from Miami to Key West. This largely two-lane road consists mostly of bridges which connect the islands along the chain.

The Keys are known for their wildlife, with many endemic plant and animal species including the Key deer and the American crocodile. There are many different species of dolphin and porpoise in the warm water surrounding the islands, and the Keys are home to the endangered manatee (sea cow), which is always a delight to observe. The Key lime is not an endemic plant but a naturalized species introduced from Mexico. The Keys have, however, made it their own in the form of the world-famous Key Lime Pie.

Each of the Keys has its own personality, but they all share a laid-back approach to life. Key West is the most popular of the islands with tourists, and from here many cruises and boat trips can be arranged to appreciate the natural beauty of this place. The island has an Old Town with charming colonial architecture, bars, cafés, restaurants and shops on its palm-fringed streets, and don't miss the Key West Botanical Forest and Garden for a relaxing stroll.

The San Juan Islands

The San Juan Archipelago in the northwestern corner of the continental United States is divided. The San Juan Islands are part of Washington State, whilst a second group belonging to Canada is known as the Gulf Islands. The archipelago has more than 450 islands but fewer than one-sixth are occupied and only a handful may be reached by public ferry.

The islands were initially named by the Spanish explorer Francisco de Eliza in the 1790s, but subsequent American and British expeditions in the 19th century changed many of the original Spanish names, though not that of the archipelago itself. Most of the islands are hilly, with valleys or flat areas in between. Coastlines vary enormously, with sandy and stony beaches, inlets, coves, bays and harbours. Many shorelines are characterized by the presence of

Boats moored in Roche Harbor.

POPULATION:
14,000 (2007 estimate)

WHEN TO GO:
Although the islands boast an average of 247 annual days of sunshine and low rainfall, winters can be windy and chilly, so they are an ideal May-September destination.

HOW TO GET THERE:
Lopez, Shaw, Orcas and San Juan (usually in that order) are reached by ferry from Anacortes. Guemes Island also has a ferry service from Anacortes. Fly to San Juan by light aircraft from Seattle.

HIGHLIGHTS:
Orca-watching from Lime Kiln Point State Park on San Juan Island (May to September).

The panorama seen from the highest point in the San Juan Islands, Mount Constitution on Orcas Island – said to be the most impressive view in Puget Sound.

Shark Reef Sanctuary on Lopez Island, a completely natural park with sensational cliff-top sea views.

Total tranquillity on Shaw Island, where the only commercial operation is the general store run by the Franciscan Sisters of the Eucharist.

YOU SHOULD KNOW:
Some lesser San Juan Islands can tell their own story – for example Barren Island, Cemetery Island, Justice Island, Picnic Island, Skull Island, South Finger Island or the Wasp Islands (named after a ship rather than the insect).

gnarled madrona trees, with pine forests often covering much of the inland area.

The four main San Juan Islands are San Juan itself, Orcas (the largest), Shaw and Lopez. Nearby Guemes is small, with limited facilities. The islands serve as an important tourist destination, easily reached from booming Seattle, much appreciated by those who love the sea, unspoiled nature and the great outdoors. Principal activities are hiking, sailing, kayaking and orca-watching.

But the islands are well organized to serve all the needs of visitors with numerous facilities such as museums, galleries, boutiques and restaurants to be found, especially on San Juan and Orcas. The towns are small but welcoming – historic Friday Harbor on San Juan and Eastsound on Orcas head the line-up, supported by numerous villages and

The shore of Jones Island at sunset

hamlets full of character.

For those who can afford it, the very best way to visit the San Juan Islands is by seaplane, with views to die for all the way (be sure to get a window seat).

241

Santa Fe

Nestled in the picturesque Sangre de Cristo Mountains, Santa Fe was planned around a central plaza, according to Philip II of Spain's 'Laws of the Indies' in 1573. The north side of the plaza is home to the Governor's Palace, to the east is the church, now the Cathedral Basilica of Saint Francis of Assisi.

In 1912, in an effort to establish tourism, it was decreed that a single style of architecture should be used across the city to promote a unification of the varied styles that had been built through the town's history. Local officials decided on the Spanish Pueblo Revival look, inspired by the defining features of local architecture: *vigas* and *canales* from the old adobe homes, the churches found in the pueblos and the earth-

An elegant Santa Fe restaurant lit up at night.

WHERE IS IT?
112 km (70 mi) south of Taos.

WHEN TO GO:
Santa Fe enjoys 300 days of sunshine a year, but temperatures are most hospitable in spring and autumn. It is beautiful in mid-September when the aspens in the surrounding mountains turn yellow and the skies are clear and blue.

HIGHLIGHTS:
The city is a mecca for artists, it is not far from scenic Taos and there's also a local ski area.

DON'T MISS:
A fun time to visit is during the annual autumn Fiesta to celebrate the 'reconquering' of New Mexico by Don Diego de Vargas, a highlight is when Santa Feans burn Zozobra, a 15 m (50 ft) puppet also called 'Old Man Gloom'.

toned, adobe-coloured exteriors. By 1930 this was broadened to include the 'Territorial' style and white-painted window and door pediments.

The city is a well-known centre for the arts, reflecting its multicultural character. Outdoor sculptures ranging from Baroque to postmodern include many of Saint Francis and Kateri Tekakwitha.

Canyon Road, east of the Plaza, has many art galleries, exhibiting an array of contemporary south-western, indigenous American and experimental pieces. The city's art market is the third largest in the United States, after New York and Los Angeles.

Artists have long flocked here, capturing the natural beauty of the landscape, the flora and the fauna. Georgia O'Keeffe's museum is devoted to her work and associated artists or related themes.

Santa Fe's major museums include the Museum of New Mexico, the Museum of Fine Arts, the Museum of International Folk Art, the Wheelwright Museum of the American Indians, the Museum of Indian Arts and Culture Laboratory of Anthropology, the Institute of American Indian Arts Museum and the Museum of Spanish Colonial Art.

One highlight is the Loretto Chapel. Commissioned in 1872 by Bishop Lamy, it was designed by French architect Antoine Mouly in the Gothic Revival style, with spires, buttresses and stained glass windows imported from France, but he died before completing the stair to the choir loft. The Sisters of Loretto did not wish to use a ladder and prayed for nine days for St Joseph to intercede. A shabby stranger appeared, offering to build the staircase if they gave him total privacy. After three months, using only a square, a saw and some warm water, he constructed a spiral staircase of non-native wood. Not only was this work impressive, the 6-m (20-ft) staircase was constructed without nails. Before the stranger could be questioned, he had disappeared. The mystery of his identity, as well as his construction techniques, has never been solved.

Lake Tahoe

One of the United State's most beautiful landmarks, Lake Tahoe's shimmering waters span 19 x 35 km (12 x 22 mi). With nearly 300 days of sunshine a year, and the surrounding majestic Sierra Nevada Mountains, Lake Tahoe offers stunning scenery and a multitude of things to do.

The second deepest lake in the US and the tenth in the world, it has a maximum depth of 501 m (1,645 ft) and an average depth of 305 m (1,000 ft).

Lake Tahoe is host to year-round activities. North

Water rushes into Emerald Bay.

and South Lake Tahoe are where you will find the majority of the world-class ski resorts. North Lake Tahoe is home to some of the ritzier and more upmarket neighbourhoods and resorts including Alpine Meadows and Squaw Valley USA, home to the 1960 Winter Olympics; South Lake Tahoe is the most populated area, with larger high rise resorts, some excellent skiing areas such as Heavenly, and also several casinos.

East Lake Tahoe is virtually undeveloped, but West Lake Tahoe is focused on residential areas, smaller hotels and inns and a variety of dining options featuring gorgeous views as their backdrop.

One of the most scenic areas to explore in the south-west is Emerald Bay, one of the most photographed natural locations in the United States. With its amazing views of the mountains, the lake, and Tahoe's only island, Fannette Island, Emerald Bay State

Lake Tahoe is one of the United States' most beautiful natural landscapes.

Park serves as a stunning backdrop to Vikingsholm, a striking reproduction of a Norse Fortress commissioned by a wealthy Chicago widow. Accessible only by boat, this folly is considered to be a fine example of Scandanavian architecture. Turrets, towers, intricate carvings and hand-hewn timbers were used to recreate the fortress. The turf roof, with its living grass and wildflowers, is like those used in Scandinavia to feed livestock in winter. Many of the furnishings that Mrs Knight desired for Vikingsholm were of such historical significance the Norwegian and Swedish governments would not grant export licences, so she had them copied down to every detail.

Whether you are interested in hiking or camping, skiing or snowmobiling, being pampered at a spa, eating gourmet cuisine, or picnicking while watching live Shakespeare – there is something to fulfill everyone in this area of incredible beauty.

WHAT IS IT?
A spectacular lake surrounded by the High Sierra Mountains.
WHERE IS IT?
In northern California on the Nevada border.
WHEN TO GO:
Lake Tahoe offers year round fun – January through March has world-class skiing and June through September has the best watersports and hiking trails
HIGHLIGHTS:
An alpine resort area, it is home to casinos, with opportunities for skiing, hiking and sailing on one of the world's most stunning lakes.
YOU SHOULD KNOW:
Indian Love Call, *The Godfather* and *The Bodyguard* were all filmed here.

San Miguel de Allende

POPULATION:
139,000 (2005)
WHEN TO GO:
Any time of year.
DON'T MISS:
A trip into the desert in the wet season (August to October), when the cacti are in bloom.
A trip to see the hibernating Monarch butterflies in January.
The Sanmiguelada bull run in September.
St Anthony's Day (17th January) when people take their animals to church to be blessed.
YOU SHOULD KNOW:
The city was designated a UNESCO World Heritage Site in 2008.

Founded in 1542 by the monk Fray Juan de San Miguel, San Miguel el Grande was an important point on the route that brought silver from Zacatecas. It was renamed after General Allende, a national hero in the mid 19th century. After a period of decline during the first half of the twentieth century, it became a popular destination for American visitors, partly because of its beautiful architecture, which the long-sighted national government had chosen in 1930 to declare a national historic landmark in order to save it. Even today, the historic centre is free of neon signs and modern buildings, and wandering round its little cobbled streets is a fantastic way to spend a few

hours, especially as restrictions on traffic are being brought into force.

The city is centred on the 'Jardin', the old town square. It is dominated by several old buildings, including the Templo de San Rafael Church and the Parroquia de San Miguel Arcangel, a beautiful 17th–18th-century Baroque church with a neo-gothic tower added in the late 19th century. According to rumour, the architect copied the design from postcards of European cathedrals. Next door, the Casa de Allende is a perfect example of the style of building favoured by Spanish nobles here in the 18th century.

The streets of the areas around the 'Jardin' have long been popular with painters and if you get here, you'll see why.

BELOW: The pretty cobbled streets of the town

NEXT: Everybody loves a Mariachi band!

Havana

POPULATION:
3,710,000 (2006)
WHEN TO GO:
Any time of year.
DON'T MISS:
The beaches.
A show at the Tropicana.
A concert at the Gran
Teatro, a fabulous Baroque-
style building.
The Museum of the
Revolution – ironically, this
opulent building was
formerly the presidential
palace of Batista and is
now a museum housing
such items as Fidel Castro's
boat and the clothing worn
by Che Guevara when he
was killed.
The National Museum of
Fine Arts.
The Hemmingway Museum
– housed in Hemmingway's
former home, this museum
documents the author's life
and works.
YOU SHOULD KNOW:
Che Guevara's 1960
Chevrolet is in the
Automobile Museum.

The capital of Cuba, and for centuries its largest and most beautiful city, Havana's architecture – although its splendour is somewhat faded – gives a unique record of colonial buildings from several different centuries, from the defensive walls and the fortress of El Morro via the grand neo-classical houses in French or Spanish style and neo-baroque buildings such as the German-style Gran Teatro to the Art Nouveau Capitolio and Art Deco in the Edificio Bacardi.

The importance of the old city (Habana Vieja) and the fortifications were recognized in 1982 when they were inscribed on the UNESCO World Heritage List. Because of the country's political isolation, the historic areas have not been invaded by fast-food chains or identikit coffee shops, and they are all the better for this. In some places, the dilapidation veers from the picturesque to the pitiful, but even then it manages to be photogenic. Government-funded restoration programmes are managing successfully to bring buildings back into use without ruining their character.

The city's links with and importance to the region's trade with Europe are evident in the many treasures in its wonderful museums. Havana is the last place one would expect to find a marble bust of Marie Antoinette, but she is in the Museum of Decorative Arts, along with Meissen, Sevres, Imari and Worcester porcelain, English landscape paintings and furniture, Chinese screens and more than 33,000 European paintings. Among the other 50 or so museums there are those dedicated to fine arts, Afro-Caribbean religious artefacts and Arabic and Asian arts. The must-see museums, however, are the Museum of the Revolution, the former Presidential

*Classic American cars,
left over from the fifties,
are all over Havana.*

Palace, and the Hemingway Museum.

But Havana is not just about its beautiful buildings and its museums; this city and its people have a vibrant character, as you would expect from a nation whose national drinks are rum, daiquiris and the mojito and whose national dance is the samba. Even though poor in material terms, Havana's near-five centuries of existence have made it rich in history, music, culture and food.

Blue shutters rest on balconies of run-down apartments over Plaza Vieja.

The streets of Havana abound with colourful characters all of whom can be photographed – for money of course!

255

The Blue Lagoon

Instantly recognizable as the paradise where Brooke Shields was ship wrecked with Christopher Atkins in the 1980s film, *The Blue Lagoon*, the swimming hole by the same name lies just outside Port Antonio, Jamaica.

This is an unspoiled oasis where you will feel as though you are the only remaining person on earth. Here the magnificent turquoise blue and emerald-green waters are an astonishing 56 m (185 ft) deep. Created by underground mineral springs fed from the Blue Mountains, it is one of the last remaining truly tropical paradises on the island. The spectacular cove is surrounded by lush, steep hills, which complete the dreamlike setting.

While swimming in the Blue Lagoon you will feel streams of warm water at times, and streams of cold water at others. There are parts where the water is shallow enough to walk right in, some with steep slopes and others with only slight slopes. You can even watch as the mineral water bubbles through the ground.

On the nearby banks there is a restaurant with a dive shop that rents out kayaks and scuba equipment.

A relatively unknown attraction, the Blue Lagoon is one of the definite 'must sees' of Jamaica and in fact the world.

The Nearby Somerset Falls are also worth a swim. This peaceful retreat is off the beaten track, so it takes an adventurous spirit to find it, but if you go for a short stroll through the wooded surroundings, you can take a canoe trip down to the crystal clear falls and take a relaxing swim in this quiet haven.

WHAT IS IT?
A large, deep, stunningly beautiful cove.

WHERE IS IT?
Near Port Antonio, Jamaica.

WHEN TO GO:
The weather is fairly consistent, with daily temperatures a tropical 30°C (86°F) during the day and 20°C (68°F) at night. Rain is moderate and occurs throughout the year.

HIGHLIGHTS:
Its emerald-green and azure crystalline waters.

YOU SHOULD KNOW:
This is where Brooke Shields and Christopher Atkins swam together in the film of the same name, *The Blue Lagoon*.

Swimming in the magnificent tropical paradise that is the Blue Lagoon.

Barbuda

Barbuda is one part of a three-island state with Antigua and Redonda, located in the north-eastern Caribbean. An unspoiled paradise of seemingly endless stretches of white and pink sandy beaches, Barbuda is surrounded by the deep blue Atlantic Ocean on one side, with its driftwood and sea-shell strewn wild beaches, and the calm clear waters of the Caribbean Sea on the other. Undeveloped except for a small number of boutique resorts, Barbuda is perfect for swimming and snorkelling, with plenty of opportunities to see turtles and tropical fish as well as some interesting shipwrecks that lie undisturbed in the turquoise water.

A short trip from the nearby island of Antigua, Barbuda was first settled by British and French, unsuccessfully until 1680 when Christopher Codrington

Eleven Mile Beach on Barbuda's west coast

began cultivating sugar on the island after establishing a British colony large enough to survive the ravages of nature and the local Carib population.

For much of the eighteenth century his sugar plantations proved a successful industry, the island's prosperity rivalling that of its larger neighbours. The Codrington family influence can still be seen in the island's street names and architectural remains.

The ruins of the Codrington's Highland House lie at Barbuda's highest point (38 m (124 ft)) and on the island's south coast sits the 17 m (56 ft) high Martello tower and fort used both for defence and as a vantage from which to spot valuable shipwrecks on the outlying reefs.

The population seems to largely consist of the more than 5,000 graceful magnificent frigatebirds that gather on the north-western lagoon at the bird sanctuary. They cannot walk or swim and instead rely on flight for survival. They harass less agile flyers like pelicans, egrets and cormorants until they drop their catch.

Barbuda, just 24 km long and 13 km wide (15 mi by 8 mi), is largely rocky and flat, with much of the island covered in bush. It is home to a variety of wildlife including deer and boar, land turtles and guinea fowl as well as the occasional wild cat. Feral cattle, horses and donkeys wander about and sheep and goats roam freely in the village, returning to their pens at night. There are several salt ponds where it is possible to see a wide array of birdlife, and there are many caves to explore in the area surrounding Two Foot Bay. On one of these caves there are ancient cave drawings and in others it is possible to climb right through to the top of the Highlands from where you can see for miles. Other caves go underground and underwater requiring expert knowledge for exploration. Darby Cave, a 45-minute walk from Highland House, is an extraordinary example of a sink hole where, in very dry weather, the salt ponds sparkle with crystalline sea salt.

WHAT IS IT?
An idyllic tropical island in The Leeward Islands.
WHEN TO GO:
November to April is the best time to visit.
WHERE IS IT?
A 20-minute flight or a 3-hour boat trip from Antigua.
HIGHLIGHTS:
Pristine white and pink sandy beaches, coral reefs and shipwrecks. Beachcombing, golf, tennis, snorkelling, diving, sun-seeking and relaxing.

Seven Mile Beach

WHAT IS IT?
Coral-sand beach.
HOW TO GET THERE:
Scheduled flights to Owen
Roberts International
Airport.
WHEN TO GO:
All year but the drier
months of December to
April are high season
NEAREST TOWN:
George Town
DON'T MISS:
Snorkelling in Stingray City.

Seven Mile Beach is a crescent of immaculate coral-sand beach running along the western shore of Grand Cayman, the largest of the three Cayman Islands. The beach is world-renowned for its translucent aquamarine water, huge expanse of fine white sand, glorious sunsets, scented air from the Australian pines that grow in the hinterland and an ideal average winter temperature of 27°C (81°F). Not surprisingly, it recently received an award for being the 'Caribbeans' Best Beach'.

Although a consequence of its outstanding natural beauty is that it has become the most developed part of the island, this has its advantages in that there is something here to suit all tastes in the way of bars, restaurants, hotels and entertainment. There are extremely strict environmental laws to prevent the beach from being ruined by building development and it is so spacious that it feels remarkably uncrowded.

Seven Mile belies its name, being in fact only 5.5 miles (9 km) long and it is becoming progressively smaller due to constant erosion by the sea. However, it feels endless as you walk along this outstandingly beautiful stretch of shore, especially in the evenings when you can watch an amazing orange sun going down over the sparkling ocean, reflecting its colours in the darkening water. The whole beach is public property and you can walk its entire length unhindered. It has a completely relaxed atmosphere with few restrictions on behaviour; only nudity is forbidden. The unpolluted clear sea is superb for both swimming and snorkelling with many off-shore reefs to explore, teeming with radiant tropical fish among the corals. Seven Mile is the epitome of the ideal beach holiday.

*A couple walking along
Seven Mile Beach.*

Mustique

This privately owned tropical island, the 'Gem of the Caribbean', is renowned as a playground for the privileged. It is less well known that Mustique is a protected nature reserve and offshore conservation area of incredible beauty.

The 5 km (3 mi) long, 2 km (1¼ mi) wide island in the north of the Grenadines, was once used to cultivate sugar but was abandoned in the nineteenth century and allowed to revert to its natural state. The rolling hills, with panoramic views, are criss-crossed with nature trails. From a height of 150 m (495 ft) you descend through forested valleys to immaculate white coral-sand beaches and limpid turquoise water. The many sheltered coves around the island were once favourite hiding places for pirates and are a natural habitat for frogs, lizards, iguanas and crabs. The whole island is a profusion of flora and fauna. Even the island's airstrip is in a forest of bougainvillea and palm trees, with terns, herons, sandpipers, and frigate birds flying overhead. There are over 50 indigenous bird species including the Mangrove Cuckoo and Tropical Kingbird.

Mustique was once owned by Lord Glenconner, who famously gave a ten-acre plot of land to HRH

Princess Margaret as a wedding present in 1960. Today the island is owned by the Mustique Company Ltd, a consortium of island homeowners set up specifically to protect the island from the ravages of property development. There are fewer than 100 villas, most of them available for rent, and only two hotels. Around 500 people live permanently on the island and, even at peak season, the island population is never more than about 1,300. A perfect balance has been struck, so that the island is habitable at the same time as retaining all its natural tranquil beauty.

Brightly painted wooden 'lace' decorates the facades of a pair of colonial-style cottages.

263

Eleuthera

Eleuthera is the Greek word for freedom; and it was in search of religious freedom that the island was accidentally colonised in 1648 by Captain William Sayles and a group of Puritans from Bermuda. The shipwrecked adventurers found a haven of peace, cleared of its original Lucayan Indian inhabitants by Spanish slavers, and rapidly developed their settlements along its 145 km (90 mi) of curving bays, offshore cays and natural harbours.

Here are the oldest, and still the prettiest townships in the Bahamas. Pastel green, blue, pink and yellow houses with white picket fences and gingerbread fretwork crowd stone quays; miles of pink and white sand beaches glisten into the distance; and the lush plantations of pineapple, and smallholdings of fruit and vegetable farms stretch for miles behind the fringe of coastal palms. Yet for all its length, Eleuthera is never more than 3.5 km (2 mi) wide – and at the Glass Window Bridge, which replaced an earlier natural rock archway, it narrows to less than 32 m (100 ft) between the turbulent Atlantic and Exuma Sound.

Tortuous geology has given Eleuthera some of the world's best dive sites like the Blue Hole, the Train Wreck, the Devil's Backbone and the famous Current Cut. You might prefer the bonefishing along miles of wadeable flats, or braving fishable surf for snapper, jacks and barracuda – but whatever your particular indulgence, you'll return to Eleuthera for its natural beauty and serenity. It is blessedly free of gambling, shopping and amusement parks. Even Dunmore Town, on Harbour Island off the east coast and the heart of celebrity-dripping, upscale Bahamian chic (Versace's personal architect recently re-designed what was already called 'the most luxurious beach in the world') is full of the calm and grace that form Eleuthera's greatest asset.

POPULATION:
9,000 (2005)
WHEN TO GO:
October to June. Come for the 4-day Pineapple Festival and Junkanoo party over the first weekend in June.
HOW TO GET THERE:
By air via Miami or Nassau; by excursion ferry from Fort Lauderdale; or by the weekly Out Islands mailboat service.
HIGHLIGHTS:
The fishing village of Spanish Wells off the north coast, where Spanish galleons watered, and the locals are direct descendants of the original Eleutheran colonists.
Hill Steps in Dunmore Town, an underground tunnel cut by 18th century prisoners from the cove to a nearby house; and re-used for rum-running during the US Prohibition years.
The 1.5 km (1 mi) long, vaulted magnificence of Hatchet Bay Cave.
Fishing for wahoo in 'the pocket' between Chub Cay and The Joulters.
YOU SHOULD KNOW:
The island is called 'Citagoo' in the rural patois.

Relaxing in the shallows.

The Turks & Caicos

POPULATION:
30,000 (2007 estimate) – of which some 28,000 live in Provo and Grand Turk
WHEN TO GO:
Year round, but whale watching is only possible from December to April.
HOW TO GET THERE:
By air to Providenciales or by cruise ship to Grand Turk; then by private boat or plane charter to the other islands.
HIGHLIGHTS:
The 18th and 19th century architectural styles of TCI's original Bermudan salt merchants, along Duke St and Font St in Cockburn Town, Grand Turk.
The Molasses Reef Wreck exhibit at the TCI National Museum – it tells of the oldest European shipwreck in the western hemisphere, in 1505.
Salt Cay, proposed as a UNESCO World Heritage Site for its historic integrity.
Any of 33 protected island and marine sites totalling 842 sq km (325 sq mi).
YOU SHOULD KNOW:
Columbus first set foot on Grand Turk in 1492 – most of TCI has remained untouched since then.

Just 900 km (550 mi) south east of Miami, at the very bottom of the Bahamian Archipelago, lies a British Crown Colony which uses the US Dollar as its official currency. The Turks & Caicos (TCI) – 40 islands and cays, eight of them inhabited – are full of major contradictions. They are set round the edge of two limestone plateaus, in shallow waters that merge into mangrove swamps and refresh the salt pans on which their prosperity has depended since the late 17th century. But at either end of the group, the surrounding coral reefs give way to seriously deep water channels, and the combination has given TCI the richest ecological variety of any island group in the area.

On land you can see iguanas, blue herons, osprey, pelicans, frigates, boobies and huge flocks of flamingoes. You can share the warm water, either fishing for tuna, wahoo, blue marlin or barracuda, or diving among the turtles, spotted eagle and manta rays, octopus, sharks and humpback whales for whom (from December to April) the offshore deeps are major transit points. Underwater, the reefs of Northwest Point, the historic wrecks of Salt Cay, and the waving coral formations descending the legendary 'walls' (some 2,100 m, 7,000 ft) of Grand Turk and West Caicos are as staggeringly beautiful as the onshore natural world.

The contradiction is that TCI is much more famous for its pursuit of material rather than natural wealth. Providenciales (aka Provo), at the western end, is the most developed island, with the international airport, wall-to-wall hotels, resorts, condos and 'entertainments'. To the east, Grand Turk, the TCI capital, is now a horrific service depot for the big cruise ships. Unless you come by yacht, you'll have to pass through Provo or Grand Turk. Grin and bear it – paradise lies beyond.

The boardwalk at Grace Bay Beach

The sun sets over Grace Bay Beach on Providenciales Island

Rio de Janeiro

POPULATION:
12,620,000 (2006)
WHEN TO GO:
Spring or autumn.
DON'T MISS:
The cablecar ride to the
top of Sugarloaf
Mountain.
The sunset from Ipanema
or Sugarloaf.
Taking the tram ride
across the old aqueduct
of the Arcos da Lapa.
YOU SHOULD KNOW:
Avoid the *favelas*.

Not the capital of Brazil, but certainly its most important city, Rio is rightly one of the world's top tourist destinations. In Sugarloaf Mountain and the Cristo Redentor statue, it has two of the world's greatest iconic sights. Its fabulous beaches, music and renowned carnival celebrations add to the attraction. This is not a city for those who like peace and quiet as life is lived here at full throttle – even the beaches, such as Copacabana and Ipanema, are party zones rather than places to relax.

The Centro (downtown) area is the historic centre, and this is where the most old buildings survive and where the majority of the museums and historical attractions lie. The South Zone is home to the Atlantic beaches. Copacabana is the site of Rio's biggest New Year's Eve party and fireworks spectacular. The North

Zone has the lovely Quinta da Boa Vista park, with the former Imperial Palace, which is now The Museum of Archaeology, Ethnology and Natural History. Other open spaces iinclude the botanical garden, the Passeio Público and the Parque Lage. Not only is the landscape around the city beautiful, but within the city limits are two of the largest urban rainforests in the world. Unusually for a city, there are also opportunities for both rock climbing and hang gliding.

Of course, the most famous thing about Rio is its carnival in the two weeks leading up to Mardi Gras, when the members of the samba schools outdo each other in the extraordinary costmes they wear and how much noise they can make. During the rest of the year, the nightlife is equally special, with clubs that attract the world's rich and famous.

If adrenaline-filled fun, set against a background of samba music, is for you then Rio is the only place to go.

BELOW: Sunset at Copacabana Beach

NEXT: A breathtaking view of the city

Armação de Búzios

Two hours away from Rio de Janeiro, this beautiful city, whose name is often shortened to Búzios, sits on the peninsula of the same name. It is one of Brazil's premier beach resorts but still retains some of the charm of the fishing village and (in the more distant past) haunt of pirates and slavers that it was before the advent of sun-seeking tourists.

It has more than 20 lovely beaches, each with its own

special character and activities: Ferruda is great for snorkellers, Geriba for surfing and Ossos for people watching. There are several surf schools and a couple of dive schools that take advantage of the crystal-clear waters and good vision. In general, the east-coast beaches are the best for watersports as they face the open ocean, while the west-coast ones provide the better places for such activities as scuba and snorkelling.

This is serious celebrity territory and the prices of the best restaurants reflect this, but the sophisticated

Búzios has more than 20 lovely beaches.

Búzios still retains the charm of a fishing village.

cuisine makes the expense worth it. The shops are clustered around the Rua das Pedras and the nightlife here is among the best outside Rio itself.

Iguazú Falls

The pounding impact of nearly 300 waterfalls, with heights averaging up to 70 m (230 ft), spanning a verdant, jungle-clad stretch of 2.7 km (1.7 mi) is not quickly forgotten. The Iguazú Falls of the Iguazú River on the border of the Southern Region of Brazil and the Argentine province of Misiones, is one of the great natural wonders of the world. Taller than Niagara Falls, and more than twice as wide, Iguazú Falls makes its smaller cousin appear to be a mere gentle overflow.

Part of the Iguazú National Park on the Argentine side and Iguaçu National Park on the Brazilian side, the Iguazú Falls have been recognized as a UNESCO World Heritage Site for their ferocious beauty.

One of the highlights of the falls is The Garganta del Diablo, or Devil's Throat, a u-shaped cliff marking the border between the two countries. At 150 m (492 ft) wide and 700 m (2,297 ft) long, the fall of water over the cliff is impressive for its staggering strength and vast power. The majority of the falls lie on the Argentine side, but panoramic views are also available from the Brazilian side. That being said, the view from a boat *en route* to Isla San Martin, on the Argentine side, is hard to beat.

Iguazu Falls derives its name from the Guarani words *y*, meaning water, and *guasu*, for big. Legend has it that a god pretended to marry a lovely aborigine named Naipu who then fled in a canoe with her mortal lover. Incensed at the betrayal, the god sliced the river in two, creating the waterfalls and condemning the lovers to an eternal fall.

The Brazilian National Park of Iguaçu is home to many rare and endangered birds and wildlife that live among the five types of forests and ecosystems. On the Argentine side visitors can explore various walkways and trails, some of which lead to the precarious edge of the precipice located beneath the falls.

WHAT IS IT?
Nearly 300 waterfalls of unbelievable scope and width.

WHERE IS IT?
Iguazú National Park (Argentina) and Iguaçu National Park (Brazil).

HOW TO GET THERE:
There are frequent flights to Foz do Iguaçu from Rio de Janeiro, and other Brazilian cities, and daily flights from Buenos Aires to Puerto Iguazú, or you can take the Friendship Bridge from Ciudad del Este on the Paraguayan side.

YOU SHOULD KNOW:
The name Iguazú comes from the Guarani words *y* (water) and *guasu* (big). Upon her first sight of the Falls, Eleanor Roosevelt is said to have exclaimed, 'Poor Niagara!'

NEXT: Admiring the falls from the viewing platform.

277

ROMANTIC GETAWAYS IN
AUSTRALIA,
NEW ZEALAND,
& OCEANIA

The Great Barrier Reef

WHAT IS IT?
The world's most extensive coral reef system.
HIGHLIGHTS:
Visit Lady Elliot and Lady Musgrave islands; the loggerhead turtle nesting site near Bundaberg.
DON'T MISS:
Learning to scuba dive.
YOU SHOULD KNOW:
There is a reef tax payable.

The Great Barrier Reef on Australia's north-eastern continental shelf is a site of exceptional natural beauty stretching for 2,000 km (1,250 mi) and covering an area of about 350,000 sq km (135,100 sq mi), making it larger than the whole of Italy. It is not only the largest UNESCO World Heritage Site on earth but also contains the world's most extensive coral reef system.

The reef runs mainly north to south, passing through a number of different climates, accounting for the thousands of different species of marine life that inhabit it. It is made up of 3,400 individual reefs, including nearly 800 fringing reefs, coral islands, continental islands covered in forest, sandbars, and mangrove systems linked by huge turquoise lagoons.

The whole reef is under threat from global warming, with increasing damage to the coral itself, but it is of vital importance to the world's ecosystem, containing as it does a third of the planet's soft coral species, the largest existing green turtle breeding site, 30 different species of mammal, including breeding humpback whales and a large dugong population, as well as sponges, molluscs, 1,500 types of reef fish and 200 species of birds. It also contains fascinating Aboriginal archeological sites and is probably the most spectacular marine wilderness on earth.

The reef abounds with multi-coloured fish.

RIGHT: Coral heart off Hardy Reef

The Whitsunday Islands

The Whitsundays are the holiday destination of your dreams. Their great and simple attraction is their generally unspoiled tropical beauty – to visit them is to be greeted by an island paradise set in crystal-clear waters and fringed by magnificent reef formations.

The islands – there are 74 in all – lie just off Queensland's coast and are perfectly situated for exploring one of the truly great marvels of nature, the Great Barrier Reef. There are plenty of day cruises from different places on the islands that take you to the best places on the reef for scuba diving and snorkelling.

A few of the islands have in recent years been quite heavily developed to cater for tourism – the expensive resort on Hayman Island is reputed to have cost A$300

An aerial view of the stunning Whitsundays

million (£110 million) to build and there are tall apartment blocks and gift shops on Hamilton Island. However, most of them are still completely unspoiled, essentially little changed from the 1770s when Captain Cook sailed through and named the islands for the day he arrived there. Whitsunday Island itself, the largest in the group, is a national park, as are many of the other islands either in whole or part. Here all you will find are great white sandy beaches, secluded bays, often spectacular marine life in the warm tropical waters, dense green pine forests and perhaps the occasional basic camp site.

Several of the islands are completely uninhabited and some are still privately owned. Such is the popularity of sailing and cruising around the Whitsundays that you can often get the impression that there are more people about at sea than there are on land.

WHAT ARE THEY?
A group of 74 mostly unspoiled tropical islands.
HOW TO GET THERE:
Fly to Proserpine on the mainland, or from Sydney to Great Barrier Reef airport (Hamilton Island), or from Shutehaven to Brisbane by ferry boat.
WHEN TO GO:
Arrive between June and September for humpback whale watching.
HIGHLIGHTS:
Platypus-watching in Eungella National Park (on the mainland).
DON'T MISS:
Whitehaven Beach.

Fraser Island

WHAT IS IT?
The largest sand island in the world.
HOW TO GET THERE:
By boat from the mainland or by air from Hervey Bay.
WHEN TO GO:
Summer, or August–September to watch whales.

Stretching 123 km (76 mi) alongside Queensland's coast, Fraser Island is one of the most beautiful places on earth. Made almost entirely of sand, it is unique. Some of the dunes are up to 240 m (790 ft) high. In the lowlands, the heathlands are awash with wildflowers in spring and summer, while in the interior, ancient rainforests surround more than 100

freshwater lakes and grow alongside crystal-clear
streams. Among the highlights of the island are the
wetlands of the Great Sandy Strait, where dugongs
and turtles may be seen, and Hervey Bay during the
whale migration season, when more than 1,500
humpbacks pass through. Inland, the lakes are
beautiful, particularly Lake Wabby and the lakes round
McKenzie. The northern part of the island has been
designated as a national park. If you drive up the
eastern beach northward from the Pinnacles, you will

*The stunning colours of
Fraser Island.*

NEAREST TOWN:
Hervey Bay 15 km (9 mi)
DON'T MISS:
Lake Wabby
YOU SHOULD KNOW:
Swimming offshore is not
recommended because of
the rips and sharks.

The interior of the island is covered in ancient rainforest.

pass the 25-km (15-mi) expanse of the Cathedrals – cliffs made of coloured sand – on your way to Indian Head, which is a great spot for looking for dolphins, sharks and whales.

Other wildlife here includes what are probably the purest strain of dingos (do not feed them: they are losing their fear of humans and there have been several fatal attacks), loggerhead turtles, manta rays, possums, bats, sugar gliders, wallabies, echidnas and several species of reptile. The most noticeable of the 200 or so species of bird here are the sulphur-crested cockatoos, because they make so much noise, although the rainbow lorikeets are rather more colourful.

RIGHT: Boardwalk at Lake McKenzie

The Bay of Islands

WHAT IS IT?
A beautiful bay on the north coast of New Zealand's North Island.

HOW TO GET THERE:
By road or rail from Auckland to Russell or by air to Kerikiri then by road.

WHEN TO GO:
Any time of year.

The Bay of Islands Maritime Park's 144 islands are dotted around a bay with clear blue waters and a rich variety of wildlife. It is a paradise for sailors, a mecca for big-sports fishermen and a heaven for wildlife-watchers. Warm equatorial waters mean that it has an equable climate and locals claim that it doesn't have a winter.

The best way to appreciate the coastline of the bay and the islands is from the water, whether from a kayak, yacht, cruiser or amphibious 'duck'. For many visitors, the highlight of a stay here is the opportunity to go dolphin- or whale-watching: sightings are almost guaranteed here. It is even possible to swim with

dolphins or, rather, to go on a licensed tour, get into the water and let them decide whether to swim with you.

Among the several good dive sites is the wreck of the Greenpeace ship, *Rainbow Warrior*, which was sunk here by the French secret services in 1985, and is slowly being colonized by marine organisms. Elsewhere, the reefs of volcanic rock are covered in forests of kelp that are teeming with subtropical fish.

Local scenic highlights include Cape Brett, and the Hole in the Rock on Piercy Island, and several operators offer boat trips to them.

This is also a historic area of New Zealand: the treaty between the British and the Maori was signed at Waitangi, overlooking the bay.

NEAREST TOWN:
Russell
DON'T MISS:
Swimming with the dolphins.
YOU SHOULD KNOW:
There are strict rules about how closely boats can approach whales and dolphins.

Boats moored off Russell in the Bay of Islands.

Milford Sound

WHERE IS IT?
In Fiordland on the isolated west coast of lower South Island.
WHEN TO GO:
October to March
HOW TO GET THERE:
By car, boat or scenic flight.
HIGHLIGHTS:
Bowen and Sutherland falls, Cleddau Canyon, Milford Sound Underwater Observatory, Te Anau Wildlife Park.
YOU SHOULD KNOW:
The Milford Track is known as one of the most beautiful walks in the world.

Paddling alongside the dolphins.

Milford Sound is in Fiordland, on the isolated west coast of lower South Island. It is the best known of the fiords and sounds that were gouged out of the coast by glaciers some 15,000–20,000 years ago, and it is the only one that is accessible by road. This vast and glorious wilderness of forests and mountains, lakes and waterfalls contains some of the best of New Zealand's hiking trails.

The far end of the sound is dominated by the 1,412-m (4,633-ft) Mitre Peak, but it is the combination of the constantly changing light, clouds, sunshine, pouring rain and rainbows that make it such a dramatically beautiful place. Captain Cook famously passed the entrance to Milford Sound twice, in 1770 and 1773, without discovering the entrance, which was hidden in mist on both occasions. The sound got its name from John Grono, a sealing captain who discovered it in 1822 and

named it after his birthplace, Milford Haven in Wales.

The Milford Track is a four-day hike from Te Anau Lake, across the Mackinnon Pass to Milford Sound. It is renowned amongst hikers as one of the most beautiful walks in the world, taking in rapids, mountain passes, alpine fields, rainforest and the Sutherland Falls,
one of the world's highest. Fiordland has a huge amount of rain – 7,600 mm (300 in) per year and the forest reflects this – giant trees wreathed in moss and vines, lichen and ferns, and all dripping with water. If walking doesn't appeal, take a cruise to the mouth of the sound – you will see Sinbad Gully, a classic glacial valley that is the last refuge of the endangered kakapo, as well as seals and dolphins, even penguins if you are there in the autumn.

The sun sets over Milford Sound.

293

Aitutaki

In terms of its population of around 2,500, the beautiful island of Aitutaki is the second largest of the Cook Islands. This group of 15 islands, named after Captain Cook who landed there in the 1770s, are scattered over 1,830,000 sq km (706,380 sq mi) of the South Pacific, yet have a total land area of only 240 sq km (93 sq mi). Aitutaki was probably first settled by Polynesians in about around 900 AD and its first known European contact was with Captain Bligh and the crew of *HMS Bounty* in 1789, two weeks before the mutiny.

Does life get any better?

It is a coral atoll with low rolling hills, banana plantations and coconut groves. Along with the small uninhabited islets to the south and east, Aitutaki is surrounded by a barrier reef, thus creating the spectacular turquoise lagoon that makes it such a perfect place for swimming, snorkelling and scuba diving.

Although it is the second most visited of the Cook Islands and tourism has now become the main source of income, Aitutaki is still very unspoiled. The palm-fringed white sandy beaches, the magnificent clear sea, coupled with the wonderfully relaxed pace of life on Aitutaki contribute to making this remote island the stuff of which dreams are made.

HOW TO GET THERE:
Fly from Auckland via Rarotonga.
HIGHLIGHTS:
The old church in Arutanga; the gigantic Banyan trees.
DON'T MISS:
A lagoon cruise to the islets of Akaiami and Tapuatae (One Foot Island), flyfishing for the fighting bonefish, *ika mata* – marinated raw fish with coconut sauce or Aitutaki's dancers, who are famous throughout the Cook Islands.
YOU SHOULD KNOW:
Captain Bligh (who returned in 1792) is credited with introducing the paw paw to Aitutaki.

NEXT: Kayaking in the lagoon.

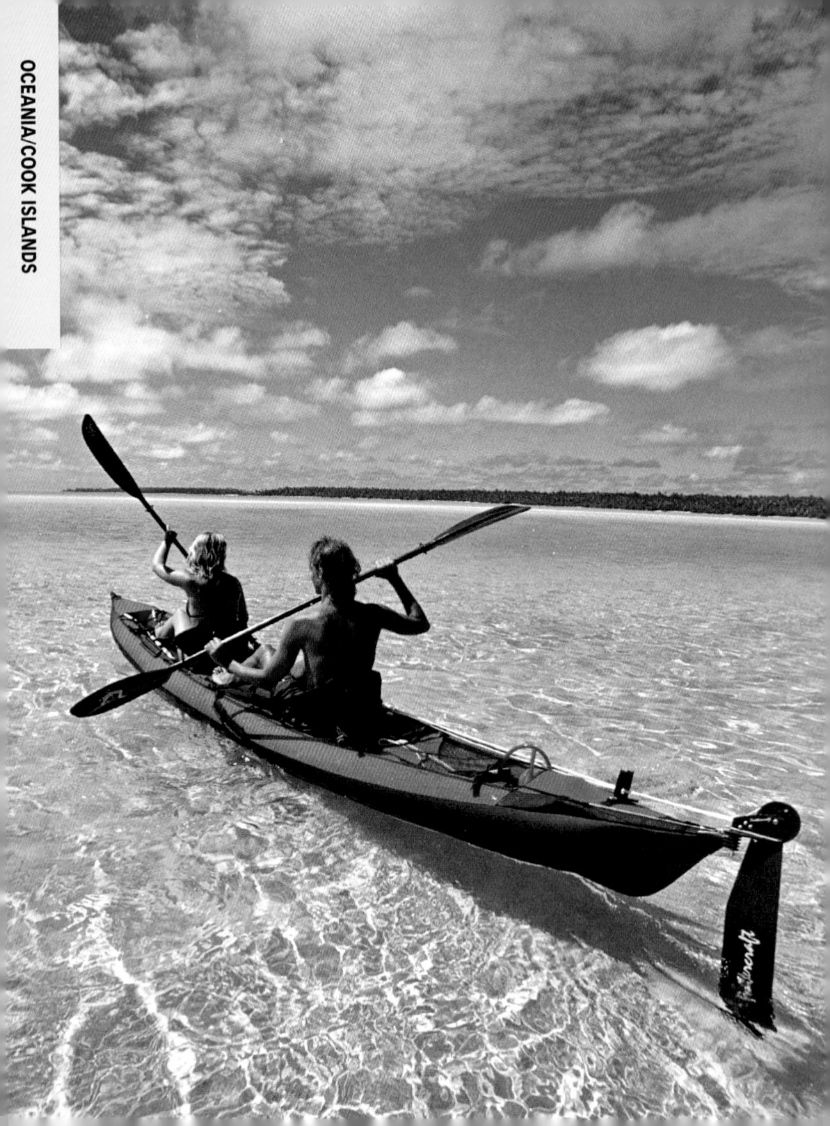

Bora Bora

OCEANIA/FRENCH POLYNESIA

One of the Society Islands in French Polynesia, Bora Bora consists of the tip of a submerged volcano almost completely surrounded by a near-rectangular reef. It is simply beautiful. The beaches on the reef have the white sand of ground-up coral, and the lagoon is the exact shade of blue that all lagoons should be. The lagoon and reefs have a bewildering array of fish, crabs, clams and eels, but the best spots to see marine life are in the open ocean beyond, where barracuda, tuna, red snapper, jackfish and several species of ray are to be seen, as well as black-tipped, grey and lemon sharks and turtles. Between August and October, humpback whales may also be seen on migration.

Every sort of water sport ever dreamed of is available in the lagoon or the ocean nearby but for the less active, the reefs, with their huts on stilts and palm trees are the ideal place to relax. Glass-bottomed boats show off the wildlife in the lagoon, while among the most popular excursions are the ray- and shark-feeding trips.

On the main island, the best way to get around is by bicycle. Other activities on offer include horse-riding and tours up to the twin volcanic peaks for lovely views over the idyllic lagoon.

WHAT IS IT?
A volcanic island in the Society Islands.
HOW TO GET THERE:
By air or sea from Tahiti.
WHEN TO GO:
May to October.
NEAREST TOWN:
Papeete, Tahiti 230 km (140 mi)
DON'T MISS:
The wonderful diving.

An aerial view of Bora Bora

NEXT: *A fringing reef encircles the island of Bora-Bora, with Mount Otemanu visible in the centre.*

Rangiroa

WHEN TO GO:
June to October.
HOW TO GET THERE:
Fly from Tahiti or Bora Bora.
HIGHLIGHTS:
The bird sanctuary on
Motu Paio.
Take a lagoon cruise in a
glass-bottomed boat to see
the wonderful corals, sea
fans and multitudinous
fish species.
The Pink Sands – at the far
south-west of the atoll, the
sands are a lovely shade of
pink, a beautiful contrast to
the turquoise lagoon and
blue sky.
The Island of the Reef – here
raised coral formations
create a dazzling tidepool
environment.
Shooting the pass of Tiputa
– here hundreds of fish,
sharks and moray eels swim
around you, swept along by
the strong currents. You
may even spot a rare black
and white dolphin.
YOU SHOULD KNOW:
The numerous reef sharks in
the lagoon will come up to
investigate but they are
nosy rather than aggressive.

Rangiroa is a stunning archipelago of 78 low islands spread over several hundred kilometres of the eastern Pacific around 200 km north of Tahiti. This is the second largest atoll in the world, the coral-encrusted rim of an ancient submerged volcano encircling an enormous shallow inland sea with more than 240 islets or motu. The motu are separated by at least 100 shallow channels and three passes, two of which are big enough for ships to enter the lagoon.

The lagoon waters are sparklingly clear, and vary in colour from jade-green to purple, a real surprise for first-time visitors. The marine life here is truly astonishing, with over 400 varieties of rainbow-hued fish glinting in the iridescent waters among the brightly coloured hard and soft corals, and the gently waving sea fans. The lagoon is understandably famous for its unsurpassed snorkelling and scuba diving, while outside the reefs there are amazing numbers of eagle rays, sharks, barracuda and tuna along the walls of the drop-offs.

The main villages in the archipelago are Avatoru and Tiputa, which offer the visitor a unique look at the South Pacific lifestyle, with their coral churches, craft centres, restaurants and tiny shops. Tiputa is situated at the eastern end. Its picturesque houses are ringed with bleached coral and flowering hedges, and nearby is the bird sanctuary on Motu Paio, well worth a visit.

There were more settlements on Rangiroa during the 14th and 15th centuries, and the remains of these can still be seen today, including cultivation pits and coral temples. To protect themselves from the aggressive Parata warriors from the atoll of Anaa, the Rangiroa inhabitants took refuge on the southwest side of the atoll. The village they created there was destroyed by a natural disaster, probably a tsunami, in 1560 and the entire population disappeared.

The Blue Lagoon at Taeo'o, an hour's boat ride from

the village of Avatoru, is a natural pool of aquamarine water on the edge of the reef, and probably one of the most idyllic places in the world. This is like a gigantic natural aquarium with wonderful colourful corals and numerous reef sharks. The surrounding *motu* are home to rare birds, including the Vini ultramarine parakeet.

Wading out to a motu in a blue lagoon at Rangiroa.

301

COUNTRIES

PLACES